Good Advice
for
Young Trendy People
of
All Ages

Good Advice

for

Young

Jennifer Blowdryer

editor

Trendy People

of

All Ages

Manic D Press

San Francisco

For Alvin Orloff
who endured two harrowing years of high school with me

Cover design: Scott Idleman/BLINK   Editorial assistance: Sierra Logan
ISBN 1-933149-02-7   Printed in the USA

Contents

The boy at Wal-Mart had eyes full of a need for adoption. I wasn't cruising him. I was gently, carefully letting him know that his tribe was out there, beyond the cinderblocks and hubcaps that filled his front yard. It took me ten years to make it to the other side of this dynamic. How many strangers had I set my eyes upon, begging for reassurance? In that moment, I wish I could have handed him something useful — something more than a smile, something more than a soft-eyed stare that said "hang in there" or "save your money."

— Kirk Read, *How I Learned to Snap*

Introduction

I was tutoring Japanese students in midtown Manhattan when Manabu showed up. He was an anomaly among the students in the corporate ESL (English as a Second Language) school, which mostly consisted of executives and housewives. Round face, bad skin, plucked eyebrows. One day he came in wearing a skirt for men, and the school's owner just about had a heart attack. Another day Manabu claimed he cut his tongue, but of course he'd had it pierced and was lying out of habit. Manabu was going to have a tough road ahead, and I found myself with an odd thought: *Please don't let me happen again.*

I understood his troubles right away, having taken plenty of blows for being ahead of trends, and I could see this happening to Manabu in the upper-class Japan of the early '90s, which socially was a time more like America's 1950s. He ended up taking Special K, ketamine, and walking in front of a bus, badly wounded in the most literal sense. I couldn't help Manabu — the culture gap was too severe — but I began to mull over the idea of providing a guidebook to help others like him: the fashion-forward and culturally isolated. Manic D Press kindly agreed with my idea, and I got to work.

You see, I'd been the first punk in high school, an ardent fag hag back when that was frowned upon, a student at Columbia University while simultaneously appearing in skin mags, a campy and blithe stylist in an era of sincere and detailed writing — all kinds of things too early for surrounding society — and taken the blows. Jazz philosopher Albert Murray, who spent his life in the Air Force in order to weather the storm of being an iconoclastic African-American critic, pointed out that "Avant Garde" is a military term. It refers to the shock troops, the ones sent to the front of the battle who end up dead or badly wounded.

Now at the age of forty, I comfortably inhabit the margins of society. I've got a smallish tenement apartment, several talented friends, and a nightlife hang-out spot. I need never talk to a square again. Since my life is no longer a desperate affair of violence and starvation, I am fortunately in a position to help others.

In the first section of this book, I urge people not to make the same mistakes as I have made. For example, I once threw out a costume and regretted it terribly; I let the threat of eviction unduly upset me instead of taking it in stride; I failed miserably as a dominatrix-for-a-day; and shed tears over my mounting debt when the collection agency bastards threatened.

None of this need happen to you. Mykel Board's chapter, "The Joy of Debt", explains how to make the most of credit cards, and Mistress Daria's advice clues us in on the lucrative career of professionally abusing the successful. James St. James, author of *Party Monster* (one of the best books of the twentieth century), gives advice for the budding celebutante, while celebrity doorman Clint Catalyst explains how to behave properly while seeking admittance to that key source of social change, the Nightclub.

Of course we all must develop our own styles from within, and I know that you are creative enough to make your own decisions. The pundits in this book sometimes contradict each other, and (much as I chose Quentin Crisp as my own philosopher) you'll have your own affinity for, say, Reverend Jen when she advises you to Take Your Hair Seriously, or Bucky Sinister when he tells you to Fuck With Your Hair. Sherilyn Connelly is strongly against plastic surgery, while Jane King extols the value of Botox. Regi Alsin, who's been incarcerated for twenty years, has some valuable tips for coping behind bars, but he doesn't mean to say that a prison term is necessary or advisable .

Even poverty is not required, as you will see in the "Jobs You Can Have" section. Nor is talent in any way essential, as Alvin Orloff reveals in his valuable tips on being a Flunky. You might breed, as contributors Pamela Holm and Ariel Gore have done, or decide to modify your gender, in which case Lynnee Breedlove and Sherilyn Connelly are here to help.

Putting an end to copious drug use can be just as interesting as drug use itself. One of my favorite wags, Phillip R. Ford, shares his rehab experience. Finally, being the Black Friend, as comedian Black Brother X tells us, need never be dull again. I'm sure there's some advice I've neglected to compile, and you, my trendy friend, may take this basic primer and run, run, run with it.

Jennifer Blowdryer

Good Advice... in General
Jennifer Blowdryer

Eviction

If you're getting evicted, do nothing for twenty-four hours. When I'm getting evicted, I dress casually for my date with Housing Court, and whine to the management company. You cannot fight with people who don't mean well. They will fight back meaner, longer, and harder. Whining is good because it delays everything; it can buy you that crucial minute. A street fighter once told me a good trick is to say, "OWWW," really early in the fight, so your opponent will think you're already hurt bad and might go lighter on you. A friend suggests saying you're Billy Idol's drummer — hard to disprove.

Open Book

I am in favor of making one's life an open book. If everybody knows you are considering going out with So-and-so, they can give you the dirt. The other option is to misstep alone and suffer silently. If everybody knows you just smoked crack, they may excuse you from the consequences of your behavior. We're all supposed to be understanding now, but you have to give us a chance to understand something first. So do tell.

However, when personal information becomes a weapon, as it is on the East Coast and perhaps Japan, the social construct is not correct. The best reaction is to form a noise band and just scream and scream (check out Sick of It All, Masonna, the Boredoms). I mean it, go see them.

Art Trap

The minute you start to care what a group of other aspiring artists think of you, it is all over. You are trapped. That group is probably no bigger than twenty-five people max, but you have no freedom now because you just gave it to them. When that group of twenty-five, or any individual in that group, starts to give you shade, just remember that life is not that unfair — their shade is not bigger than reality.

If you write an amusing book, paint a comely painting, or perform in a way that is not a total snore, rewards will come: chuckles, an exhibit in some cafe in Burlingame, future attendees. If you are young, it will all seem to matter so very much, but take it from me, Jennifer Blowdryer, it does not. Do you want me to come over right now and tell you that? Because I will. I can think of no better use of my time.

Sex Work

Many people find they cannot survive — as in eat, keep an apartment, buy textbooks — without hustling a bit. If you do find yourself go-go dancing, turning tricks, or staffing a phone sex line, I recommend writing about your escapades for *Penthouse*, *Hustler*, and *Chic*. Remember that aforementioned "Open Book" lesson, information should not be a weapon? Well, after I wrote up my experiences in a series of paying articles, my checkered past was a matter of public record and it opened several doors for me.

If you have to survive, you'll do what it takes. If you like it, you'll embrace it, especially if you are in the mutant progressive environment of a feminist-run sex toy shop. Just don't forget to announce it to the world, every last detail, because this is how we take away the shame. Remember the previous twenty-five people "Art Trap" rule? Just expand that to the fly-over states, but not necessarily your parents. And take lots of breaks.

Dangerous Wannabes

At some point in your trendy life, somebody will want to be you. Perhaps their youth was not tortured enough, or they were tortured in the wrong way, and they are not enjoying your modest success. It's just like in this movie you should see, *All About Eve*. These people will compliment you winningly, and that will progress quickly to shadowing you. It's kind of nice to have a flattering little shadow around, isn't it? But watch out. It's not just that they want to become you, but that they don't want there to *be* a you anymore. Ironic, isn't it? But so are most human machinations.

If you're a writer, they might write something similar to what you write, but not as good. If you're a singer, they might dress like you and go for your lover. If you're a visual artist, I don't really know exactly what they'll do as I can't draw very well, but I'm sure it's all similar. Even if you just have good outfits and are popular at bars and parties, I guarantee, you'll meet your Eve.

The key thing about these Eves is that they are spiderish and spin a sticky web: they will go through your friends, talk about you, and get paranoid delusions about you at some point which they'll immediately share with somebody dangerous like the accountant who cuts your freelance writing checks. It seems they can't just be like you; they must wipe you out in the end. There are probably a lot of well-known artists that began their careers as Eves who succeeded in doing this.

These Eves are on the wrong track. *Only lies are dull*, says Quentin Crisp. And these Eves are, ultimately, rather dull. If, for example, they worked their own style talking about how their uncle stuck his finger up their ass when they were eight and that is why they are so crazy, it would be perfectly interesting. However, that is much too original for them. They have mutated and must act like someone else, say, Henry Rollins, instead. Admire him or not, the Western world has heard of Henry Rollins, not the Eves he's surely had: all that military dating, upper-cap text, and weight-lifting has gone down the drain for these imitators.

Just get that Eve out of your apartment. The friends who believed the Eve's version of you are useless anyway, and your Eve will fall apart, no longer able to suckle from the organism they hoped to feed off and devour: you.

Threatening Up-and-Coming Trendy People

There is a trendy rule I'd like to invent right now: If you are threatened by somebody, learn to love them. They may just help you. That is the way to stay trendy and sane for many years, which is our goal, after all. If they are capturing the eye of your former lovers and admirers, just know that in five years time, you will both still be around, while those lovers and admirers might move, breed, or sink into an alcoholic stupor.

How did I deal with it when my German boyfriend was captivated by the lovely Jane Graham, who had a zine called *Shag Stamp* and had been a stripper in Northern England? I told her we'd know each other a lot longer than we'd know him, and I ended up writing the introduction to her book, *Floozy*. You don't have to get hurt by these new trendy people. If they are snatchy, it's just nervous reflex. You may even mean a lot to them, so be nice. They'll give you a gig one day, mark my words.

Arch Rival

At some point you will have an archrival. My archrival is named R. G. I could use a pseudonym but can barely spell that word anyway, and there would be no chance of escalation of hostilities if I used a fake name. When did it start? Why, as far back as 1989, I'd say. I was friends with this guy who liked to fuck around with crazy women, and he may have been the one that got R. going. When we arrived at a place, R. would loudly say "Here comes that clique!" She was burning up with jealousy.

Like a good archrival, though, she was also sort of like me. I might have yelled something like that if I was really sick of a clique. This guy really did get those crazy vulnerable ones all cranked up, too, practicing this sort of sexual neurotic female-baiting that guaranteed him the odd stalker. R. G. and I had more direct contact later, when I played a maid in this French surrealist play she directed. Even though she didn't like me, she was desperate and decided I'd be best in that minor part.

One night I gigged with my band at a benefit R. was hosting. R. was in front of the band with some interminable raffle, while I bitched impatiently in the background. She ran across the street to a payphone while I played, and left this great archrival message: I was like a gargoyle rolling my eyes around, didn't I know she was trying to do that raffle, I was disrespecting the other performers by even being on the bill, and what's more she knew I didn't spend $8 on a videotape of myself being a maid in that play because I was buying dope with that money. At the end of the answering machine tape, which I saved, she says she's going to bash my head in.

I sat on that tape for years — you can kind of hear my band playing right across the street in the background — and once, when I had a big show produced by HBO, I had the sound guy play the answering machine tape over a house beat. It didn't make the airwaves, unlike the time my Eve bitched on the *Jenny* show about a roommate (me, of course) who wrote about her. That was a good one, using the medium of television to continue a feud. I was scheduled on the *Montel* show as a performance artist, and was about to retaliate, but got bumped by the L.A. Riots.

We're both social misfits with no partners, R. and I, and one Christmas we were on First Avenue and Fourteenth Street in Manhattan, headed in opposite directions. We were both horrified. I meanly did not say Hi. Years later, at an open mike, the nearest rapprochement I could make to R. was to smile vaguely in her direction while making remarks that could have been inclusive. Her body was aching to drop the feud, for any gesture. It was all so useless and so very long after Victor, both the play and the man, the raffle, the maid, the dope, the threats, but I wasn't big enough to be outright friendly.

A few years ago I had a hit play, *Let's Talk About Me,* running in the basement studio of Theater Rhino in San Francisco. Running in the upstairs theater was something called *Off White Party Weekend,* by Dramaturge R.G., the poster informed me. Honestly, "Dramaturge"? What are the odds? Well, apparently, with your archrival, if you are really meant for each other, the odds are very good that you will never get away.

Oh, did I mention the time she copied my entire outfit but didn't look nearly as cute?

Things That Will Age You

A federal trial will age you. They will send seventy cops to your house, hopefully you'll be out getting coffee at the time, but they'll get you anyway. If you are not put in jail, you will be forced to stay at home watching a lot of TV, cooking stew, and having visitors. If you are put in jail you can become a gay anarchist, like Regi Alsin, and read a lot. If you're a man, get a spider tattoo on your neck. Girls like me will always go for that.

Work will age you. This can't be avoided, unless you're on SSI in the U.S., or the dole in the U.K. Just try to work with people, don't get stuck in some hole by yourself. I hear social interaction is crucial when in a work-type situation. You can tell anecdotes, make little jokes and generally work on your conversational patter. When I used to work with people, checking coats or teaching, I would try on different personalities and attitudes — coy, brisk, authoritative, clownish — and I think the teacher voice I developed has helped me out of a couple of jams.

Having a firm indignant voice often buys me that minute to get away. Guys with chains who wanted to throw me and my friend out of a vintage Buick were surprised when I popped up and said, "Just WHAT do you think you're doing?!!!" Sometimes that voice snaps people out of their violent fugue state, and they will stop beating up your associates.

The sun will age you. Try to just go out at night, early evening at the soonest. As the sun gets worse, the poor will be stuck outside, and the better-off will have air purifiers, lodging, and sunblock. This doesn't mean you have to wear a floppy golf hat, however. Those hats only look good if you weigh about eighty pounds.

Non-Productive Celebrities

If you're interested in gold-digging, you must study the Gabor family: Magda, Eva, Zsa Zsa, and their mother Jolie. Now, a lot of things that happened before you were born, wars and suchlike, might not be that important but the Gabor sisters are really great. They started out in Hungary. Jolie kind of raised them to be married, but I'm not sure if they were fortune hunters or just survivalists.

Jolie entered Zsa Zsa in a beauty contest when she was fifteen, and got her a reputation as a beauty. They actually all had pleasing faces, but stumpy legs which they hid by constantly wearing gowns. Zsa Zsa's father, Vilmos, tried to ban her little Scotty dog from the house, so at the age of sixteen Zsa Zsa eloped with a wealthy Turkish foreign affairs minister, who reluctantly agreed to let her keep the dog.

Zsa Zsa liked to marry, A LOT.

Magda, the oldest sister, drove a Red Cross ambulance during the war, helping Polish soldiers to escape Nazi persecution. She stayed in Hungary until 1946, after helping rescue some 5,000 soldiers. During WWII, the other two Gabor girls married quickly and hit the States, and in 1945 their mother joined them, opening the Jolie Gabor Pearl Salon on Madison Avenue in New York City.

Eva married the fewest men, only five, which is nothing compared to Zsa Zsa's nine. Swindlers always seem to slip up and marry another swindler at some point, and Zsa Zsa ended up with Prince Frederick von Anhalt in 1986, who eventually inherited a couple of castles.

Zsa Zsa once starred in a movie called *Queen of Outer Space* which was an incredible piece of camp-within-camp. Her only direction was, "Try not to laugh at the dialogue." Amazons in short skirts run the planet, but Zsa Zsa, as queen, gets to wear — you guessed it — a gown. Zsa Zsa was mostly known for her snappy talk show comments, and if you're going to be a non-productive celebrity, I suggest you also work on your zingers. Here are a few Zsa Zsa nuggets: "I believe in large families: every woman should have at least three husbands," "I don't take gifts from perfect strangers. But then, nobody is perfect," and, "How many husbands have I had? You mean, apart from my own?"

Zsa Zsa's still alive and batty: a few years ago she slapped a traffic cop in Beverly Hills, then was arrested. She did the right thing — talked to the press of the free world, like that time Sophia Loren went to jail because Carlo Ponti didn't have the right I.D. Zsa Zsa claimed to be worried, at the age of seventy-something, about the lesbians in jail. Leona Helmsly also complained about the big lesbian scare when she got a jail term in her sunset years, but that's another story.

Eva Gabor was the most talented of the Gabor sisters. She was the platonic female companion of Merv Griffin, who misses her terribly, and she and Zsa Zsa were frequent guests on his talk show. There's a '60s television sitcom you might not have heard of, *Green Acres*, in which glamorous Eva, wearing gowns, had to live right near a pig sty. That was kind of the entire joke, and Eva really made it work. She missed Park Avenue but was married to a cute guy, Eddie Albert, who just had to live on a pokey farm with laughably hickish neighbors. Instead of washing dishes she threw them right out the window, and the biggest joke, one the show never tired of, was her unspeakably bad cooking. Eddie might pretend to like it and then retch, and the hick neighbors would cringe. Eva should just not have been on that farm when she adored Park Avenue so.

Trust Fund

Hide it in liberal college towns and cities like San Francisco where down-at-the-heel bohemianism is still chic. Flaunt it in glamour spots like LA or New York.

Whenever I hear somebody is the Colgate or Mead Notebook heir, it makes them glamorous to me. It's not that I think I'm going to get any of that money — one seldom does — but the corporation has a movie-star charisma to me. After all, those corporations do run the world.

If the trust-funders have any character flaws, my advice is to just get used to them. Without that specter of the sidewalk as their potential home if they screw up just one more time, they can screw up indefinitely, and live out everybody's secret dreams: firing therapists when they get too personal, taking Xanax when they feel a little hinkey, and generally being a well-dressed terror. All the rest of us can do is remind them to give their cast-offs to charity, feeding the great thrift store god that has given so much unto us.

Washington D.C.

Don't act too crazy in Washington D.C. — they'll put you in an institution. There is a woman in Los Angeles called Celestyne. She got semi-famous by paying for her own huge Hollywood billboard, sporting a classic starlet platinum hairdo and huge tits. Sounds harmless, right? Well, according to her former personal assistant, she is not. She forges checks, hooks with intent to harm, runs scams, and is impolite to her personal assistants. Celestyne is an entity in Los Angeles, allowed to thrive in between the occasional arrest. In Washington D.C., she would be locked up for good. I choose L.A.

Family

I was born, weren't you? Sorry to all you New Age devotees: I did not choose my parents nor that big appointment with a hospital in Northfield, Minnesota, circa 1961. Quentin Crisp says the thing with parents is that you hate them but you need them, and I agree that you do need them for your early years, when nature makes us as cute and seductive as possible to guarantee we'll be fed, not just left in a ditch somewhere.

Speaking of family, are all those wretched holiday reunions really worth the money you expect to receive some day? You might not get that cash anyway, so just choose the relatives you like, or none at all. Try to get through life with the most painless acquaintances possible. I don't even consort with strangers who bug me.

Documentation

Always put the year on flyers for shows, gigs, and parties. You may be young yet, but believe me, you will host, appear in, and emcee more events than you ever thought possible, and when looking through your cute storage box many years later, you'll have no idea when you did what. Try to save every piece of documentation, because you will move a lot and then be left with about seventy percent of what you did, if you're lucky and don't have a fire. For some reason, we trendy people seem to have a disproportionate amount of fires — I think it's our candles and the antiquated wiring in our vintage lamps — so try to get a metal filing cabinet. I had my first little candle fire on a wooden bureau in Rhode Island when I was about fourteen, trying to create some atmosphere stuck in the middle of nowhere.

Ideas

You might have about one good idea a year, and that will be stolen. People don't mean to steal it, unless they're Eves, and it's hard not to be upset when it ends up on a hit album or sitcom. I think of myself as having an organic trend antenna: it's not like I'm exactly THINKING of these things, they just come to me before sweeping the country or at least a small crowd of eighty with-it people.

My good ideas? Well, let me see, my SmutFests were copied by a promoter I worked with, and he straggled on for years with Sin City, Sex Party, all these less catchy names. White Trash Debutante? I came up with the term in a San Francisco parking lot. Roseanne used the catchy phrase on her show, and a band under that name is still plodding away in California, with a rotating cast of hundreds. I could be a bitter old barfly, crowing about all this, but that would be tired.

Mental Illness

Now, I don't have manic depression, but you just might. A lot of trendy people do. Even if you don't, you will have friends who do — that's part of the package. Where others run for the hills, you must become a fan of the colorful personality disorder. There is just too much good material there to miss. Here's the rundown on bipolar disorder symptoms, so you'll know if you or your friends have it: Money-making schemes, paranoia, inappropriate sexualizing of practically everything, spending sprees, animated charming behavior rotated with crushing down periods. People with this condition don't always take their meds, because apparently it's loads of fun being on a manic high, and they miss that, as anybody might. Plus when they're in their conspiracy mode they might think their counselor is getting graft on the government supply of Lithium and Welbutrin, or something like that.

I personally love manic depressives, but I don't recommend working for them in their mad, cluttered studio apartments. Their own form of chemical imbalance is not suited for management capability and they cannot focus enough to train their parakeets, which may peck little scars on your wrist.

Couples

It's hard to talk to a couple, and if one of them is mad at the other, SAY NOTHING because they'll make up and unite against you.

Trendy Continuum

At some point, after you've been around a little while, you'll notice there's a younger version of some part of you running around. They are not your Eve or your Archrival, and it's a mistake to think so. They are part of the same thread you picked up from whatever album, book, or movie first got you going in that miserable backwater town you grew up in. Embrace these little yous. I am drag mother to two younger people. One didn't even know about wig caps, and I was jarred by this until I remembered that somebody had to tell ME about wig caps, somebody who was so much a part of me that I don't even remember who it was. Of course you need a wig cap, I just know that now.

Drag

Never throw out your drag, unless you're dying. Even then you can have a private little sale and invite other trendy people, so your outfits will live on and people will have a good costume for any possible future tributes to you. Think you'll never use that vampire cape again? You're wrong. Think you'll NEVER need a vampire cape, even though it's on sale? Wrong again. You need that cape, that wig, that big hat.

That Big Hat

When you wear a big hat, it creates a festive atmosphere. Strangers will perk up and talk to you. Not in the usual mean way, but nicely. When I was very young, there was no cultural context for my appearance so strangers would yell, "Rod Stewart!" at me, but now the why has changed to how: How did you get… your nose pierced? that startling hair color? that cute big hat? Wear a sombrero and you'll always have friends.

Tattoos

It's always good to have words tattooed on you when you can, so I got the word "Chaos" tattooed on me, along with a lance pattern I'd admired at the Tower of London. "Chaos" became the buzz word *du jour*. It can mean the shape things are in before they arrive at their final perfect state, lack of order, or, to me, the history of America. Amazons used to carry similar weapons to the one I got tatooed, so it is a lesbian feminist symbol while also resembling a weapon carried by two-headed dwarves in *Dungeons and Dragons*. I didn't even have to know all that in advance, it just fell into place.

If I want to soften it up I might add some kittens playfully chasing a ball of yarn around the battle-axe. Everyone loves little kittens. You can also get a Tasmanian Devil smoking a joint, or a snake. Just kidding, get whatever you want, or choose to stand out from the crowd with no tattoos at all. Be as original as you dare, or, like me, as trite as you prefer. When a tattoo artist, tired of putting unicorns on lesbians, suggested the tribal black rose I wanted would be on the girl pumping gas in ten years in Lincoln, Nebraska, my response was that I like flash (the more common designs frequently displayed on the walls of tattoo parlors). If I choose to express myself, I can simply speak. Of course, not all trendy people have this luxury, because there are…

Completely Visual People

I used to be frustrated by these completely visual people. Why the hooks dangling from their flesh, the two-toned hair, the unwieldy shoes, if they didn't want to chat? Through the years I have come to realize that visual trendy people are having a dialogue, it is just a visual dialogue, and is mainly with each other. From one fashionable person to another: once those holes close up, it's almost impossible to get a second piercing through the scar tissue on your nipples.

Turning Forty

Helen Gurley Brown says that when you're twenty-eight, everybody will still want to be around you, but after that, you have to work hard. I forget the type of hard work she suggested, although there was something in there about how to give a good blowjob. It's true that someday you will turn forty, unless you get killed in a vintage lamp fire. You have two choices: you can grow old gracefully, or hang onto youth by your manicured fingernails. I do a little of both. I am wild for new slang, and spend every second possible with parolees because they have the best new slang ever. I know now that I would be a J Cat if I'd ever been 51-50'd, and how to make money on the slender.

When you turn forty you like a different type of conversation. Personal dramas begin to be a bore, and you start warming up to the chatter like, "Mendocino had a railroad running through it? Huh! Now where did that word originate?" It's soothing. I love listening to old ladies on the bus, and want to jump the gun thirty years and talk like them immediately: "My, that was interesting... certainly was...," but of course I'll have to wait (and also make sure I have friends when I'm seventy).

I like to dress somewhat youthfully, but realize it's too late to jump on the eyebrow jewelry train, although that seems to be on the wane anyways. There are limits, such as no baby tees, and raver pants would just look silly. I prefer to hang onto the trends of my relative youth, a look I formulated at the age of twenty-five or so. This was not my formative trend — which was punk rock — but, at forty, one transitions from the spiky to the flattened stud. Take that anyway you like.

It's fun to hang around young people, but one mustn't lunge at them. Also, your problems and brand of therapy-speak may fall flat with the very young, from whom one has no right to expect the understanding nods of a paid professional. You must lead workshops, or at least have loads of opinions to impart.

How to Be an Art Star
Advice from Reverend Jen

Eliminate Hobbies

Everything an art star does should be done with obsessive/compulsive zeal. As an Art Star, you should have one goal in life: to produce art. Anything that interferes with this should be eliminated from an Art Star's existence.

To take an example from my own life, it wasn't enough for me to simply collect trolls. Instead, I opened a Troll Museum. I was still able to engage in the gratifying act of collecting trolls while at the same time finagling my way onto Japanese and Spanish television, the WB evening news and the pages of the *NY Times*, thus exposing those who lead normal lives to the Art Star way of life, and with any luck, giving hope to disaffected, bored youths living in the suburbs. Not to mention, the act of giving tours of my museum to visitors is performance art unto itself. If you're thinking of collecting Legos, by all means go for it, but make sure you do something obsessive with those Legos. Why not build a giant Lego hut and attempt to live in it for a week? Or, as I saw one young girl had done, build a giant Lego memorial to a deceased pet, and put pictures of it online for others to view. This brings me to the second rule of Art Stardom:

Carry Through on Even the Craziest Ideas

You might be sitting at a bar with a friend discussing Teletubbies and you might say, "Wouldn't it be fun to dress as a drunken Teletubby and visit various toy stores throughout the city?"

Or you might be discussing the commercialization of Christmas and your friend might say, "It would be great fun to dress as a pregnant Virgin Mary and go to various fancy hotels trying to get a free room on Christmas Eve!"

A true Art Star wouldn't just talk the talk, they'd walk the walk, and the next day they'd go out and have a Teletubby or a Virgin Mary costume made. Or they would make it themselves, and they'd make these ideas a reality. Art Stars live in the land of show-me.

Avoid Self-Improvement

Unless you plan on learning an obscure language like Elvish, avoid self-improvement. Self-improvement is for people with time on their hands, and Art Stars have no time on their hands. An Art Star should have no spiritual life and no sense of who they are. Who an Art Star is and what they believe is something other people called critics will find out long after the Art Star in question is dead. It's okay to dabble in religion in order to observe the strange customs of non-Art Stars, but that's as far as it should go. Art is an Art Star's religion. It's that simple.

Practice Dating as "Performance Art"

Nothing will sap an Art Star's art-making energy faster than a serious relationship. So, date only as a form of performance art. Date people who fascinate you, not people who appear to be boyfriend or girlfriend material. You can save a lot of money by dating a crazy, fascinating person because you don't even have to go out. Just listening to the delusions of your crazy date will be entertainment enough. Not that Art Stars need entertainment. Art Stars entertain themselves.

Be Fashionably Early

If you are invited to a party that offers an open bar and the party is scheduled to start at 8:00, be sure to get there at 7:59 and no later. There is no sense in pretending that you are there for the party when all you care about is the free booze and food.

If you are an Art Star who is in recovery and can't drink, go there for the food and stand right next to the kitchen so that you can snag the hot hors d'oeuvres as soon as they are available, sparing them from the hands of partygoers who can afford to eat dinner.

Only Take Jobs that Offer No Room for Advancement or Personal Growth

The last thing you want is to get roped into a job that will prohibit you from staying at open mikes until four in the morning five nights a week. That's why I recommend taking the crappiest job you can find. During the Web boom of 1999, the Art Star community flourished because hundreds of Art Stars found easy jobs that paid exorbitant wages. As for me, I had a job as an "information architect", which meant that I surfed the Web eight hours a day, four days a week, and did almost no work. This was the perfect job because I had Internet access and was able to send out press releases for my one-person shows from my desk. Looking back, it's no wonder most start-up Web companies did nothing but lose money, as so many of them had Art Stars squandering their time and money.

Try to find a crappy job where you have access to a copy machine and a fax machine. These two items are essential to furthering one's career as an Art Star. With a copy machine, one can make flyers, books, posters, etc. With a fax machine, one can send out press releases in bulk. Do accept raises, but don't accept promotions. A promotion means more work and no Art Star wants more work.

Learn to be poor. Learn to conserve. Learn to love pasta. Find a vintage clothing store where you can trade in old vintage clothes for new vintage clothes so that you always have a fresh, exciting wardrobe without having to spend money on one, and without having to get a promotion to pay for it.

Get a Strange-Looking Pet and Name It After Yourself

That way if you die, you leave behind a tiny four-legged Art Star as your namesake. Don't bother having kids, as they will only turn out to be computer programmers in order to infuriate their Art Star parents. A pet cannot rebel against you. In *The Satanic Witch*, Anton LaVey suggests that neophyte witches obtain a pet to act as a "familiar," a creature with whom they can share their secrets and spells. Art Stars also need a familiar on whom they can practice their one-person shows, monologues and dances. It's important to get a strange-looking pet so that you can incorporate it into your art in photographs, films, and comic books. Being an Art Star is sort of like being a superhero without the super powers, and all superheroes need a sidekick. Art Stars are no different. Most importantly, an Art Star's life is filled with constant rejection and a pet offers the opposite: unconditional love and companionship. Being an Art Star means living a wild roller coaster ride of a life. A pet is often the only stabilizing factor in an Art Star's life.

Take Your Hair Seriously

It's fine if you want to wear elf ears, platform shoes, wacky hats, or underwear over your outerwear, but don't joke around with your hair. You still want to get laid and having a silly haircut ensures that this will never happens. Even though fashion isn't a very important element of being an Art Star, as many Art Stars dress in a dull or unfashionable manner, you still need to consider it. A signature style is never a bad thing.

Revere Alfred Jarry

Alfred Jarry was the original Art Star. The author of *Ubu Roi* was of midget stature, had owls for pets, wore hooded cloaks and women's blouses, and died an alcoholic failure at the age of thirty-four. Despite this, his legacy inspired the Dadaists who inspired the Surrealists who inspired both the Abstract Expressionists and the Pop artists, creating a chain of Art Stardom that can only be destroyed by the apocalypse. Alfred Jarry lived a life of no compromise, breaking down the barriers between thought and action, and art and life. He is proof that the greatest Art Stars sometimes never become stars at all, even after they die.

Write Filthy Gossip About Yourself in Local Bar Bathrooms

This bit of advice might not seem that crucial, but once you scrawl your first bit of filthy self-aggrandizement on a local bathroom wall, you will be amazed at the far-reaching consequences. There are hundred of bars out there and that means hundreds of free press quotes all pertaining to your remarkable skill as a lover. However, don't overdo it! You want to be considered a local legend, not a local tramp, and a little "Rev. Jen sucks it good" can go a long way.

Have Fun

If you're having fun, you probably don't need this handy list of suggestions, as you are probably well on your way to becoming an Art Star. There is an innocent fervor with which true Art Stars approach life, like children engaging in an advanced form of play that separates them from people who are simply "making stuff." If you're not having fun, ask yourself, "What do I really want to do?" And then do it. Being an Art Star means figuring out exactly what you want to do and then doing it, even if it is absurd, illogical or ugly. In simpler terms, "To thine own self be true." If you've got that down, there's nothing left to teach you.

How and Why to Be A Trendy Flunky
Advice from Alvin Orloff

Being shy, I never quite imagined how I could be part of a trendy scene. Though I craved that glowing in-with-the-in-crowd feeling, I could barely summon the courage to speak, let alone sparkle, at hypersocial places where trendiness happens, like nightclubs, art openings, readings, rock shows, or protest rallies. I noticed that trends feed on publicity, which in turn feeds on flamboyance. Successful trendies are a bunch of larger-than-life "personalities" who live in and for the limelight, prancing across life's stage like ham actors mugging for an invisible camera. I would have resigned myself to life amongst the terminally un-hip, but quite by accident I discovered the back entrance, as it were, to the trendy universe. I discovered how to be a trendy flunky.

Let There Be Flunkies

First a lead singer, then a performance artist, and finally a club promoter, were all delighted to have me as their unpaid personal assistant. For some weird reason, the sort of brilliantly creative and visionary minds that drive the trendy world tend to be wildly, er, (oh, how does one put this politely?) disorganized. They need help. And though I am probably not even competent enough to work in an office, I am at least capable of typing up lyrics, addressing and mailing six hundred invites by Friday, or discussing career moves with budding superstars while they pose for press photos. I flourished as a flunky. And in return for my services, not only did my trendy masters take me to the best parties where I met all the VIPs, but I was also sometimes even in charge of giving them drink tickets! Never had I dreamed such glamour could be mine.

Codependence & Groveling

Now, not just anyone can be a flunky. Codependence may be a character flaw, but for the flunky, it's a career requirement. When a trendy somebody says something true, the flunky must never nod solemnly and say "I agree," he or she must produce an obsequious grin and squeal, "You're right!" There's no corresponding diplomatic way of saying, "You're wrong," because it's not the flunky's job to rein in his or her trendy master, no matter how deluded. After all, delusions are just artistic vision with bad PR. If your trendy master sounds crazy, he or she could as easily be on to the Next Big Thing as on the way to the loony bin. There's no telling. And, I'm sorry to report, if it's the latter, you must simply go down with the ship. This may sound like a lot to ask, but recall that flunkies get to be part of the zeitgeist without ever having to give interviews, set foot on stage, or be the subject of scathing exposés. That ought to be worth something.

How May I Become a Flunky, Please?

"OK," I can already hear you begging, "I'm sold. What now?" The good news is there are never enough flunkies to service the grand ambitions of the trendy, so you don't have to hitch your wagon to any old superstar; you get to pick and choose. Flunky jobs are always hiring, and if you want to go the informal route, just hang out somewhere "happening" and be ready with the phrase, "Would you like something from the bar?" In no time some grasping, climbing, aspiring trendy person will demand your services. Before you start, though, I would suggest you peruse this brief field guide to see which kind of flunky you'd like to be.

Handy-Dandy Field Guide to Flunkydom

Assistants This group includes gophers, aides, interns, and other positions that answer directly to the whim of a "somebody". Assistants slave away for little or no money, but often exercise actual creative control. Andy Warhol, trendy somebody *par excellence*, was famous for letting flunkies run his magazine, direct his films, and even paint his paintings! Be forewarned though, history will give credit for the assistant's genius to the trendy somebody.

Hangers-on The hanger-on has almost no responsibility. He or she just needs to be permanently on-call to pad out an entourage. Duties include laughing at bad jokes, fetching drinks, and perhaps (if your somebody is a pugnacious, alcoholic celebrity) throwing a few punches now and again. Benefits include occasionally finding oneself in the background of celebrity magazine photos identified as "and friend."

Stylists Interior decorators, hairdressers, and fashion designers can often find that rare thing: a well-paying flunky job. Rumor has it Jennifer Lopez goes nowhere without an entourage of twenty, one of whose sole function it is to see that her eyebrows are well-groomed. Benefits include being first to hear all the celebrity gossip!

Henchmen Since flunkies surrender their personal judgment, they're easily talked into illegal activities. But being a flunky doesn't put you above the law. Don't wind up a "patsy," i.e. don't be a henchman!

Acolytes Gurus, priests, and such-like are invariably far too busy communing with the cosmos to take care of earthly matters like proselytizing on street-corners or the day-to-day running of their cult compounds. For these mundane tasks they need acolytes. Unfortunately, these positions often require that one wear a robe.

Groupies, Gun Molls, and Girl Fridays The specifically girl-type flunky positions are really quite antiquated and to be avoided in this, our modern age of gender equality.

Wisecracking Sidekicks This is the apex of flunkiedom, the ultimate right-in-there-but-not-in-the-spotlight position. Their responsibilities include providing moral support when their trendy somebody is down, and delivering zingers to enliven the conversation. There are no drawbacks to being a wisecracking sidekick.

Livin' La Dolce Vita

I will leave you with the caution that a career as a flunky will not win you prestige, or even grudging respect. Our winner-take-all society exalts only those who stand at the top of their chosen pinnacle, on their own two feet, singing their own special song. Flunkies are denigrated as worthless apple-polishers, loathsome brown-nosers, or pathetic toadies. I say, who cares? Even if we are at the bottom of the totem pole, we're still part of the swirling, whirling Dolce Vita of trendy society, which sure beats sitting home twiddling one's thumbs.

How to Be A Good Dominatrix
Advice from Mistress Daria

For this section, I went straight to the top. Domme Daria, currently of NYC, is a world-class Domme who's abused stars of the stage and screen. It's one thing to turn to this work in a desperate hour of need, quite another to be a talented and sought-after pro like Mistress Daria. Here she imparts her wisdom to the groveling masses.

General Tips

Give a cool name to your dominatrix character, one that reflects your sensibility and is marketable. You *do* want to make some money, after all. If you dominate with great energy and enthusiasm you will make a lot. I was always really good at making the male species cower.

As a child I would make the boys on the block play Dog with me. I walked them on leashes and made them do tricks. Oh, I was funny!

Invest in a Killer Wardrobe

Take it slow because fetish wear is expensive. Check with other pro dommes to see if they're selling any clothes. Buying second-hand leather is even better than buying it new; not only is it already broken-in, it's good for the environment and for cows. A starter outfit, or uniform, will consist of stockings, garter belt, leather or patent leather stiletto pumps, leather skirt and top. Remember, you will be meeting quite a few fetishists and admirers who live to buy you exquisite gifts.

Regarding Clients

You will need a healthy amount of fear and caution, but you must also be confident and be prepared to accept that anything can and will happen. Once, I threw open the dungeon door to meet a client, and what I saw sent a razor-sharp shiver down and up my spine. It was dressed head to toe in a clown get-up, big floppy shoes, crazy-ass John Wayne Gacey makeup, red nose, and a colossal yellow, red, purple, and green baggy unitard. I did not run, but I was extremely cautious as he also had a huge, scary hook in place of a right hand and he was holding a dummy with his left, performing a ventriloquist act. After I made sure the hook was plastic, we got to talking. His fantasy was to soak my feet in a bath of Rice Krispies, blueberries, and milk. We both marveled at the intense sound of the snap, crackle, pop, and I couldn't believe how luxurious the happy mixture felt bursting between my toes. Afterwards, he put on a big clown bib and drank the cereal footbath, every last drop.

Another client came to me with a bottle of olive oil, five packages of Oscar Meyer wieners, and an enema bag. After that session, I never ate another hot dog again, ever.

Take what you can from your clients without getting emotionally invested. Underneath our chain mail and leather, we dominatrices are still human, and what human doesn't like being adored? I once had a client who was not only handsome and a good listener; he gave me exquisite jewels, chocolates, and flowers. He even took me to the doctor when I was sick. It turned out he was married with three children. Don't fall for clients!

Always carry a safety scissors into your sessions, especially if you're playing around with auto-erotic asphyxiation. There is always a margin for error, and error here means death.

Transform your client into a slave who will emerge better for his experience with you, and you will emerge transformed and more beautiful as well. If you take another's power by force, you are not strong. So if you don't know how to do edge-play like asphyxiation, cutting, branding, piercing, or extreme bondage with sensory deprivation, don't do it. Stick to the S/M sampler of spanking, role-play, light bondage, and nipple torture.

Exploit your men through monetary gain. Every time he wants to be your ass-fucked, sissy-slut, punky-purple-lipstick-wearing slave-bitch ashtray, screaming, "Mistress, may I please have another hard-boiled egg up my ass?!" charge him for it. Watch him melt and place gifts of money and more onto your altar as you hiss the words they so love to hear, "On your knees now, bitch, and worship me!"

Regarding Art

See the human body as a canvas for your unique brand of artistry. Like Japanese Zen painters, you must contemplate each mark you plan to make beforehand; there will no way to erase it. The most powerful tool is not your whip, but your mind. All sex begins with the brain. You must manipulate your slave into a sensual, sexual object, regardless of his looks. There will be times when you'll wonder how you'll get through an hour with the hairy, smelly, broken-down, drippy-dicked little man kneeling before you. Let your mind rule your senses, not the other way around.

Keep a Journal

Your memories may be worth something some day.

Door Etiquette for the Nightlife-Challenged
Advice from Clint Catalyst

My foray into nightlife as a form of employment harkens back to ancient times. It was the summer of 1994, and the club kid "phenomenon" was teetering on its final pair of pink seventeen-inch platforms when I arrived in San Fransicko, CA. I was young, dumb, and eager, and quickly made a name for myself among clubland cognoscenti due to the ridiculous amounts of time and energy I funneled into my "nighttime looks." These qualities may not be worth the price of photocopying on parchment paper, but they fit the criteria for work within a realm that requires no resume: nightclubs. As the adage goes,

California is a sunny place for shady people — but when that blazing orb is out of sight, the personality types get so dark, they nearly eclipse humanity.

In my ascent from genderb(l)ending go-go boy to club host to guest-list guru and finally to Gatekeeper/Cash Box Bitch and part-time promoter status, I've accumulated a few tricks of the trade (double entendre intentional). I'm here now to share my secrets and offer some good advice for how to go about your "going out."

Bring ID

This should be a given. Even if your hair is gray and your face a fan of wrinkles. Just do it. As soon as you don't, there'll be a problem, and the last thing anyone wants to do is trudge back home over a stupid laminated card with an unflattering photo

Bring Cash

It doesn't matter if you're on the list and best friends with the bartender, or plan on "using your card to open a tab." It also won't cover coat check, that hit of ecstasy that serendipitously presents itself, or the tips you need to tuck in a hot new go-go dancer's g-string. Stash at least an emergency twenty somewhere, honey. Accidents happen, especially with comp lists. Promoters and club personnel have a lot on their plates, and, whether blinded by bling-bling or thrown off course by the incessant bling bling blinging of cell phones, names can fall through the cracks. It's rare that a venue will let you cover a door fee on your card.

Guest List

And when your turn arises to hear those chilling words, "You're not on the list," handle the situation with dignity. Screaming and physical threats are appropriate on *Jerry Springer*, not at a locale where peops are trying to look their best. If you're dissed at the door, do something revolutionary: be polite. Admittedly, saying, "Thanks for checking," doesn't do much to ease your embarrassment, so if the first option leaves you feeling less than satisfied, another thing you could do is make an amicable joke. If it's a guy who was supposed to put you on the list, quip that he must not have found the blueballs funny after all. If it's someone of the female persuasion who left your name off, muse "Oh, well I guess this means we're breaking up." The latter is particularly amusing if it's evident you're homosexual. You know how we gays are: a real laugh riot.

What *isn't* funny, however, is making a joke along the lines of, "There's three of us — can we get a group discount?" or "It's after midnight. Shouldn't we get in for less?" Bartering is an at-your-own-risk activity. Your best bet is to save it for the flea market. It bugs.

Oh, and another thing: street cred is non-transferable. In other words, spare telling the door staff how important you are in another town. So you're a big deal in Portland or Poughkeepsie? Good for you. Either stay there and relish your Big-Fish-in-a-Toilet-Bowl glory, or cough up the cover charge like any self-respecting tourist. If you really *are* important, the $12 door won't matter. Getting into clubs for free does not a celebrity make, sweetness. In fact, there've been plenty of losers on my guest list: panhandlers who mistake themselves for artists, drug dealers, deadbeat roommates of friends who called in a favor, and SSI superstars who shoplift for sport.

If star treatment is the route you want to go, flashing a studio laminate or business card won't work on a jaded queen like me. Don't strut to the front of the line with five friends in tow and hand me a glossy rectangle that states that you work for Capitol Records. All that does is remind me you're in a much higher tax bracket and are completely capable of paying everyone's way in, let alone your own. Instead, butter me up with some good old-fashioned swag. If you work for a label, bring me a stack of promo CDs. If you're a hairdresser, offer to do my color for free. You're a barista at Starbucks? Cool enough. I'll take some comp coupons to cover my daily caffeine dose. The Gatekeeper post may look like a throne, but we're not above bribes — any of us. I mean, let's face it: this power exchange isn't about heart-felt friendship, it's about bullshit. So don't embarrass either one of us and pretend we're old buddies. Just skip the big talk and shuck out the kick-backs. I'll remember who you are next week and impress your dim-witted pals. Promise.

Speak Loudly

Not only does it make you seem boisterous and self-aware, but it also serves a practical purpose. If the staff have been employed in this club a long time — say, like three years, which to these folks feels like forever — they're hard-of-hearing. Or, if they're wise and intend to prevent "Huh?" from being their general response for the remainder of their lifetime, they're wearing protective ear plugs.

Read

If you've made it this far, this one shouldn't be difficult for you: READ. If signs are posted stating "No Ins And Outs" and "If You Leave,

You Have to Pay to Get Back In", guess what? You really *can't* go to your car to pick up your inhaler (why would you go somewhere notorious for cigarettes and smoke machines without it anyway?) or that alleged "emergency tampon" you know you could swipe from a drag queen primping in the ladies' room, and you really *can't* go "check to make sure you didn't get a parking ticket." Are "No Parking" signs ever tentative?

Remember that just about any clever excuse you concoct to conceal the fact that your cheap ass wants to go swig bargain booze in the car is probably more worn-out than those Diesel distressed denims. Spare the door staff your game of Will-I-Or-Won't-I-Be-The-Big-Exception, and either stay in the club or sashay somewhere else. As with anything, there are exceptions. I once let down my guard for a girl who told me she'd just been dumped and needed to go to the car to fingerbang some of her frustration away, but that's because I've got a soft spot for the heartbroken who still retain their wit.

Dress Code

Soft spot or simply over it — some door whores are way harsh with the dress code, but I'm not even going to embark upon your outfit. There's a time and a place for everything, including chartreuse stirrup pants on men, gold Guido chains and chest hair on women, and plastic forks used as transgender fashion accessories. Ditto that with the other thing you're gussied up in: attitude. Nightclubs are an illusory realm where ordinary people can act like movie stars and celebrities can pretend they're ordinary people. Part of the plan is knowing a club's scene or theme, though ultimately this is a matter of personal expression.

So you didn't like the club? It's part of the trial-and-error process.

Count your losses, catch a cab, and head somewhere else, but *don't* pester the counter crew for a refund. When you go to the theater and don't like the movie, do you expect to get your money back? If you do, my guess is you've got few friends who want to participate in public activities with your chintzy self. Don't mistake the club door for the customer service counter at Wal-Mart: this is one place where the customer is *not* always right and your satisfaction is *not* always guaranteed.

Oh, and whatever you do, don't fight with the security guards. Even if a couple of pals jump to your defense, there's more security staff on board. They back each other up and club management backs them up; they will win, and you will be humiliated. I've seen a television actor wailing in tears and flopping around on the floor, a handcuffed idiot, all because his alcohol consumption and ego led him to believe he was such a hotshot that he "could take a security guard on." Not only did he fail miserably, but he also had a hipster audience to gawk at his fall from grace. Folks may forget the name of the last series he starred in, but they won't *ever* forget that night. And even if you're a complete unknown, they'll give you a tag-line like "That Drunk Queen Who Kicked a Security Guard in the Shin and Stood Crying Outside Club Cherry" to go with your face. Know how I know this? I was that drunken queen.

The harsh reality is: as unreal and "make-believe" as the nightclub façade can be, in many ways it's an accurate slice of how the world really operates. Who you are, whom you know, who knows you and what you mean to them, determine how you're treated. This isn't fun information to bandy about, but get some perspective, honey. *Please.* Unlike some of the other injustices in the world, if you don't like club politics and power, you don't have to participate. There's great freedom in that fact.

I've given advice for how to get through the door; now you're on your own, pal.

The Art of Working a Room
Advice from James St. James

Now you, too, can conquer any scene in high style! Watch as uppity faggots fall into line! Semi-important people think you're a Somebody! Has-beens cling to your coattails! It's easy! It's fun! It's the patented Brill-o-matic 1-2-3-4 to Social Acceptance!

First: Spend at least six hours getting ready. Study yourself in the mirror at home. Is your hairdo media-friendly? Will your outfit read in black and white? Does your "look" inspire at least two clever sound bites? Remember, you must be eye-catching but simple. If you and your "look" can be reduced to a simple caricature and not lose any essential qualities, you've got yourself a hit. Think Carmen Miranda, Jessica Rabbit, or the members of hair-metal band Poison. Be sure that your partner doesn't clash with your look. Plan ahead and execute together.

As you stand outside the entrance to the party, take your partner by the hand and shake it once for solidarity. Quickly, adjust your vibrations to the music. Throw your ears back, push your energy forward, turn on that smile and SWEEP into view.

Enter the room in a clatter of commotion.

Circle the room once together, smiling and saying hello to EVERY PERSON in the room, even and ESPECIALLY if you don't know them. Pretend that you do. You should make a snappy comment about something they're wearing like, "My, what a beautiful corsage!" (if it's a woman or a drag queen) or "Darling, look at those massive shoulders!" (if it's a man or a drag queen).

Smile and acknowledge EVERY PERSON in the room... in a clockwise rotation — never stopping, never pausing — always moving, always smiling... brilliant... animated... ON! This takes twenty to twenty-five minutes.

Then: separate! Both of you circle, alone, in opposite directions. You continue moving clockwise, your partner retraces your last circuit. Pretend you are searching for each other — that it's a matter of life and death — and be sure to involve *every person* in the club in your desperate hunt. This should take no longer than twenty-five minutes. Finally, regroup and scream with transcendental bliss at the thrill of finding one another again.

Now, lock arms and work the whole room again, telling all your new friends, "Not to worry, we've found each other at long last!"

Then leave. Never stay longer than an hour and a half on the very outside. I MEAN IT! Always leave them wanting more.

Do this every night for three months at the hottest club in town and I personally guarantee that, for the rest of your life, you will know everybody in every room of every party, everywhere.

Not Raising Cain
Advice from Pamela Holm

Dressing your Baby

Babies aren't just huge responsibilities, they can also be squirming avenues of expression, small kinetic art projects, the perfect outlet for your blistering creativity. Dress your baby in the way that you'd dress if you were that size — one-piece jammy suits, short sundresses worn with frilly underpants, fringed cowboy outfits, superhero capes, jackets with cat ears sewn into the hoods, faded corduroy overalls with lamby appliqués.

Take advantage of this fleeting moment of ultimate control. Enjoy the fact that your child is still able to skim under the fashion radar, and that they haven't yet developed enough sense of self to curb your creativity. Enjoy it, because the moment they become old enough to catch on that they've been being used as an art project, they'll have you shopping at the Gap for clothes that will blend them into the masses.

What to Do When Your Child Doesn't Want to Shop at Thrift Stores Anymore

Maybe you're of the economically challenged class or maybe you simply hate setting foot in a shopping mall, but your child is no longer up for the thrill of the thrift store treasure hunt and is tired of dressing like an extra in a '70s Blaxploitation film. Now it's time to take your child trawling for play-dates in the tony part of town. Visit playgrounds where the sandbox is always clean and crackheads aren't asleep on the slides. Make friends with the bored rich mamas whose children are slightly larger than your own. Chances are they'll think you're colorful and invite you back to their mansions. Your child will be invited to swank birthday parties, and once the wealthy get wise to her secondhand wardrobe, they'll be first in line for hand-me-downs.

What If They Want to Listen to Queen?

If your child comes home with a Queen CD — or anything else that you reluctantly lived through firsthand — and plays it over and over until you want to dust off your sledgehammer, calmly tell them a story. Tell them about the time you snuck backstage at the Queen concert trying to meet Freddy Mercury but ended up sleeping with some Scottish roadie in the tour bus somewhere between Pittsburgh and Philadelphia and had to panhandle to get enough money for a Greyhound ticket home. Your kid will be so creeped out at the thought of you having sex, with anyone really, that they'll forever associate Queen with your sordid story and trade the CD in for something else. Repeat as necessary.

Discussing Your Personal Past and Present

Nothing will keep your kid on the straight and narrow like hearing the messy details of Mommy and Daddy's good ol' days. By telling them the truth about your crash-and-burn glory times you'll practically ensure that your child will rebel against you by heading off to college and getting a real job.

Coming Home to a Houseful of Drunk Teenagers

Don't panic, don't get angry, and don't start drinking with them. Do assess the damage — check the bathrooms and showers for lightweights asleep in their own vomit. Carefully coax the wobbly ones away from the china cabinet. Check your bedroom for wayward teens making awkward attempts at sloppy drunken sex. When the party winds down pull out all the extra blankets, sleeping bags and pillows and announce that the slumber party has just begun. Explain the difference between a slumber party and an orgy. Devise a home sobriety test and administer it to anyone who tries to leave the house clutching a pair of car keys.

Raising a Decent Human Being

Children need only two things: a lava lamp and a set of lawn darts… no, wait… love and respect. Treat your child like a burden and a monster and they will rise to the occasion. Treat your child as if they are someone you actually like and they will behave in a likable fashion. If you respect them, they will respect you. Simple.

What to Do When Your Child is Embarrassed by You

The first time your child is embarrassed by you make sure to congratulate yourself — it means you're right on track. The only way a child knows who they are is by knowing who they aren't, and who they aren't is you.

On Being A Hip Mama
Advice from Ariel Gore

First things first: Get all those urgent tattoos before you get knocked up — the ol' tattoo gun is counter-indicated during pregnancy.

Next thing: Have your most fabulous fag friend organize a crazy-beautiful extravagant shower, and register! Extended family and childless friends are shockingly generous when the first kid is on its way. It's not until your rugrat starts shitting at their parties that they get crabby — and remain crabby — for some twenty years. I don't mean to scare you here, but you're embarking on a period of your life during which ninety percent of your otherwise loving, tolerant, community-oriented allies and lovers are going to feel free to dump all of their mother-issues on you like every day is Big Garbage Day. Develop a thick skin, and at once. You are doing the most important work in this world, doing God's work, if you can think of it that way; the opposite of waging war isn't waging peace — it's welcoming the newcomers to this planet with all the love and fierceness you have in you. Rock on, breeder chicks.

My Daughter the Neo-Prep

Back-to-school shopping and what does my fourteen-year-old daughter want for her first days at high school?

"Polo shirts that I'll wear collar-up, miniskirts and ballet flats!" Ballet flats? I can't even remember the last time I thought of ballet flats.

"Might as well get some penny loafers and pegged pants while we're at it," I reply.

"How do you know about those things?" she asks, like I've secretly been watching the Teen Fashion channel. I used to wish my kid had remained the punk she was at eleven, but it's not like life would be much different. The punk kids from her school now just shop at Hot Topic at the mall instead of Abercrombie & Fitch. It's just as expensive, and comes with just as flimsy a version of the original philosophy behind the fashion.

It's been twenty years since I first dyed my hair purple and started a new school year surrounded by girls in polo shirts they wore collar-up, miniskirts, and ballet flats. Is there really no new subculture? I take comfort in the fact that the '80s did go away for twenty years.

I am not the teenager anymore, I tell myself; put those years out of mind, defer to her. I say no to the body alterations all teenagers seem to want: butterfly tattoos, skin-cancer tans, piercings in easily infected places, boob jobs. You have to commit to an identity for at least five years before you can start cutting your body up over it. Besides, the ballet flats will probably end up in the free box, along with the purple hair dye — impermanent.

Jobs You Might Have
Advice from Those in the Field

I always had a hard time finding a job, though of course it was because I had not yet harkened to my true calling, that of being on SSI while flourishing as a low-level promoter, performer, and writer of important books such as this one. There are a few avenues open to you: hairdresser, bartender, tattoo artist, panhandler, and yes, medical test subject.

Bartender

For this section, Jim Flynn interviewed one of the best, Moonshine Shorey, of the NYC Bowery Poetry Club and Coney Island's Sideshows by the Seashore.

I treat the bar like a stage. The way you make the best money is to treat it like a performance. People always say you should go to bartending school, but I just fell into this. It's always a friend calls and asks to help out. You make sure that the people have the best time, and that money gets into the register. You are the babysitter of the liquor, but remember, it's not your liquor.

Customers

Sleazy Guys They like to show their money, but they don't necessarily want to spend it. They always want the best deal possible. They love to talk about themselves. One day, I had just been in Kmart to buy some underwear and saw this really nasty shirt, and later that day this guy at the bar was wearing it and making this big deal that his shirt cost $300. I kept my mouth shut; I'm not into making someone feel bad. If the shirt made him feel like three hundred bucks I'll let him have that. They're kind of like the gay clientele. They'll whisper sweet nothings into your ear, like, "Can I get two more, Babyface?" They're suave in a greasy way that I kind of admire.

Hipsters Hipsters like to think that they're in a place that hasn't been discovered, that's unique. They always need to feel like they're out-of-place, but ahead of something. They think they're trailblazing, but the road's already been paved. They like drinking the cheapest beer and wearing designer shirts. It's really hard to get money out of them.

Butch Dykes Butch dykes will walk into the bar and lay down a twenty, leave it right in front of you on the bar, and then when there's one dollar left, they'll get up and leave. However, they can sit and drink a lot, so you try to make them feel appreciated. I think a lot of butches don't feel appreciated.

Artistic Types I enjoy the artistic clientele. It's not about slinging drinks and screaming. We lost a bartender because she would be better off working at a place where her tits should be hanging out. Artistic types tip here and there; it all depends on how they're feeling. Artists end up spending all their money at once. If you catch them with money, they'll give it all to you. If they're broke, they'll want free drinks all night.

The Hip Hop Crowd Hip hop parties are the worst for getting tips. Jersey people are tacky and gross, but they'll tip and keep drinking. But if it's just the real hip hop scene, they'll tip you a quarter.

Buy-Backs It's a fine line between being very generous and making sure enough money gets in the register. I'm not afraid to charge people full price even if they've bought a lot of drinks. Sometimes I'll dock money if they've been assholes. I had a friend who worked at this club, and people would say, "Give me a half-shot of this and a quarter-shot of that," and he would end up charging them $23. Come on — it's not "Pick your own pizza." I pour with a heavy hand, but in NYC, you have to be liberal with the liquor. Sometimes a shot here is $8.

Clubs

I hate working at clubs. It's the best money, but you're just kind of a machine. You don't make the connection. It's the most annoying thing on earth when people wave their money at you, but when you take their order, they don't know what they want. Annoys the fuck out of me. Know your order, especially when I'm busy.

Career Advice

If you want to be a bartender, lie. Tell them you've worked at millions of places. I got my first job when I was sixteen. I started out bussing tables, and then they had me barback. I ended up filling in for the bartenders. My mom bought me a book on making drinks, but I think my real advantage was my Native American and Irish background. Plus, you can't really fuck up a gin-and-tonic. A lot of times I make up shit. You have to have fun with it, so it's not clinical. I'd have to say that my masterpiece is the "Moonshine Mudslide," which has about ten shots in it but tastes like Christmas. I also have the "Gator Aide" which is fluorescent. I love colors; when you see something drinkable and fluorescent turquoise, you just want to try it.

Know that everyone wants your job. Everybody thinks they can bartend better than you. That's why you've gotta have a persona. I really enjoy getting people a little sloshed. I think liquor's a great drug, and I have no problem being a drug dealer.

Tattoo Artist

Jim Flynn and I interviewed Erno, former proprietor of Erno's Tattoos, and Nate from Frisco Tattoo. Both live and work in San Francisco, though Erno has also worked on design projects for the King of Thailand.

Career Advice

Erno: Personally, I took up tattooing to get away from dealing drugs. I met a guy who got out of prison, and we ordered a tattoo kit from Chicago Tattoo Company. For about $600, we got everything that two guys need to go into the business. When the kit came, the colors looked like Easter, the gleaming machines — it just gave me a mental hard-on, and we started tattooing each other. I worked like that for a year or two, and then I worked with Lyle Tuttle in 1978 and '79. I was a good artist, but he taught me the business end of it.

The truly hardworking, sincere, and talented will stick with it. There's a million hangers-on who think that tattooing rose buds on titties all day is the way to go. If this is what you really wanna do, you should pursue it the right way by getting a good teacher. If you have real commitment and dedication, start working on yourself, then work on friends and family, and rely on word-of-mouth after that.

Nate: Don't become a tattoo artist. It's an extremely oversaturated market. The money is not what it used to be, and it's probably not what you think it's gonna be. There are shops that clock a lot of money, but they're not gonna be around for a long time. We keep our prices real. It's gonna be a long, hard road. One day you're eating chicken, and the next you're eating the feathers. Eventually, the people who went into it for the money are going to fade out, and it'll go back to being cool again, but right now, it's just not worth it.

If you do decide that tattooing is what you really want to do with yourself, you should get an apprenticeship with somebody who really knows what they're doing. Otherwise you're just gonna be doing real gnarly pieces in your friend's garage, and nobody will come to you.

Clients

Erno: A lot of young guys forget that without clients you can't make a living. The customers are the most important thing besides your ability. You've probably experienced walking into a tattoo shop where nobody knows who you are, so you get the attitude, like they won't even uncross their arms to talk to you. I was taught to be like a shoe salesman: the second customers walk in the door, it's "What can I do for you?" Instead of telling people they haven't got enough money, I ask, "Whatcha lookin' to spend?" The bottom line is, take their money and give 'em what they pay for.

Nate: I guess the hardest part is the people. I'm a real introverted artistic type, so it's hard for me to work with people. Finding out what people want makes me most impatient. There are all these factors that customers don't understand, like how the tattoo is going to hold up over time, and what colors are going to work with their skin tone. Sometimes people suggest things that aren't going to work; if they would just listen to me, they would get a solid tattoo. When people get too picky, I wanna strangle them.

Every once in a while, somebody will want a piece and I'll try to talk them out of it. Like if some chick wants some guy's name tattooed across her hands, I try to get her to think about it for a day or so. Sometimes I end up doing it anyway. It actually creates job security, because ninety percent of the time, she's going to come back and get it covered up with something bigger and more expensive. It's also good to see that the kids are giving each other these ghetto-ass tattoos with a sewing needle. After they get it together and go to rehab, they're going to be paying me to cover that shit up.

Flash You Get Sick Of

Erno: Yosemite Sam, and I'm also probably black-panthered out. All that stuff's valid, but after a while it's nice to do all custom work. Still, I feel like it's not good to talk somebody out of a tattoo just because I'm sick of doing it. You should be able to squeeze out one more that's killer — otherwise you shouldn't agree to it.

Nate: What people want has a lot to do with the rock stars on MTV. Tupac had this one cross design, and for like three years, everybody wanted that. Sometimes people walk in and they don't even have to say anything. They want the Tupac cross, we just know.

Hairdressers

When I was sixteen, I cut off my hair in a punk club, so my mother had to take me to Macy's to get it fixed. There I met Julius, who didn't bat an eye when I requested a Liberace 'do, white-silver in a modified bouffant. These people — the hairdressers — seemed like me, and though I personally couldn't get into beauty school and in fact am a slob, I believe they should be the highest-ranking members of any good social hierarchy. I talked to Princess Kennedy and Zeon, a.k.a. Jazzizi Cappucino, at SF's Glamarama, Deena Davenport's ultimate salon.

How to Begin

Princess Kennedy: When I, a gay kid in Salt Lake City, was in high school, we had Career Day and a beauty school came to do a demonstration. If you entered a scholarship drawing, they gave you a free sample of shampoo and conditioner, and I wanted that free shit. So I got chosen for this scholarship. The following summer, when I turned sixteen, my mother said I had to get a job, so I went to beauty school instead. I ended up loving it, and I've been doing it ever since.

Zeon: I decided to go to beauty school when I was sixteen and dropped out of high school. It was during punk rock times and I was always bleaching my friends' hair and giving them Mohawks and all these crazy colors. I'd always go to my hairdresser and ask for advice on how to do their hair. He would talk to me about my fucked-up life (I was working in this café with a whole bunch of thirty-year-olds). I got fed up one day and he said, "You know, you should really go to beauty school. You can do it in a year."

I went through the phone book and found a beauty school that I could go to. I got a grant and took out a loan, so I was able to put myself through vocational training at age sixteen, all on my own. If you can, you should start training in high school; you can take beauty school classes in the evening, so when you graduate you'll be well on your way to finishing up your hours. Then you'll get your license, and I recommend you begin your career by assisting in a good salon with a solid training program. Although I am now at UC Berkeley studying anthropology, I plan to be a hairdresser until I'm fifty-five.

Hairdressing Philosophy

Kennedy: We all tend to be crazy, artistic, and a little bit wild. If you like to be up on the cutting edge of style, it's an amazing profession, cuz you're gonna be one of the people that see it first. Hairdressers can be some of the bitchiest people in the world, but not here at Glamarama. It's the Island of Misfit Toys. We have to go to the dryer now.

Zeon: Hairdressing has a long-standing tradition, because as long as there's been civilization, there's been hair! Hair's really important because it makes us feel who we are, it's part of how we present and express ourselves.

In high school, lots of people identified me as a fag. They used to jump me in the hallways. That's why I dropped out and went to beauty school instead. A lot of hairdressers are queer men or women, so hair salons are a safe place for people to be who they are.

Interestingly, I give a lot of advice to my straight male clients. I work with a lot women and they tell me everything, so guys see me as a good resource to find out more about girls.

Panhandling

So you want to be a beggar? I did this as a breathy and compulsive-talking teen. I'd follow my intended targets until they paid me just to go away. Here, writer Sami Formo shares his tips and career advice for successful panhandling. I will always remember running into him on a street corner where, shivering, he was attempting to sell counterfeit Swiss Army knife-and-watch sets. Since then, he's moved on to gainful employment.

The Salad Days Panhandling can be useful in the beginning of a trendy life, but it has its limitations. One of these is age. It's best to be between the ages of sixteen and twenty-three, when it is pretty effortless to be cute and charming. That gives you seven years of potentially great panhandling. Panhandling can be a lucrative means to an end, but, like all good things, it must eventually come to a close. Remember, panhandling is merely a stepping stone to getting paid for just being you.

Wardrobe and Etiquette It pays to put on an attractive outfit that says, "Hey, I embrace my poverty but I also want better things," and to also be as friendly as possible. When you're aggressive, you just appear to be homeless, which brings us to another limitation, that of trapping one in the role of "gutter punk." Just remember: the older you get as a gutter punk, the less attractive it becomes.

Don't use children as panhandling tools; it can get you into serious trouble and besides, having children won't be trendy until much later. Having late-life babies is very chic now. Teenage pregnancy was big in the '70s and '80s but now it's just vulgar. I once had a friend who used her three-year-old to help her panhandle and it made people more angry than sympathetic. Remember, we're working sympathy here.

What to Do with All That Money The money made by panhandling should only be used for four things: 1) trendy clothes and accessories; 2) beauty supplies including hair dye, makeup and good hair product for that slept-in, "I've-just-been-fucked" look; 3) booze; and 4) drugs: heroin is a youth-preserver but only if you quit eventually. Food can be found at soup kitchens and often people will give you food instead of money, so buy food only in emergency situations, like when your blood sugar is so low you are unable to perform as a good panhandler.

It is easier for women to make money than men, so it's a good idea, if you're a guy, to team up with a girl and pool your earnings, with grand plans of travel or tattoos. Hint: If you have lots of visible tattoos, hide them. Otherwise people will wonder where you got them and exactly how you paid for them.

SSI

I have chosen the somewhat passive career of SSI recipient. I also get SSD, short for Social Security Disability — it all adds up to about $650 a month, plus food stamps, health care, and prescriptions drugs, of which I am especially fond. My main disability is that I simply cannot get up in the day. I suppose I could find a night job, but I am extremely unreliable even upon awakening. At first I am humble, grateful to get a job, but soon I become indignant and grandiose, sure that they are lucky just to have me. This process, from gratitude to scorn, takes about two or three months at which point I decide to take a lengthy vacation.

There might be something at the Anarchy Festival in the UK, or I may be missing out on good nightclubs and regional cuisine in Los Angeles, Baltimore, and San Francisco. When I get back home, having exhausted every free place to stay in these other cities, I am shocked to discover that my job is no longer there. This behavior indicates at least one Personality Disorder, according to the DSM-IV, a diagnostic bible favored by the mental health profession.

Giving me SSI is actually a pretty good deal for the U.S. Government. It would be much more expensive to keep me cooped up in jail. If, like most of our nation's poor, I had to go to the Emergency Room every time I got in a fight, experienced flu symptoms, or just felt a little bit lonely, I'd be a huge drain on the medical profession. It's cheaper for everybody to keep me right at home, reading magazines and working on my writing career.

I was lucky to qualify, if Mental Illness can ever be thought of as a boon. It used to be quite easy qualify for benefits — one merely had to get a facial tattoo or be born with the wrong gender. Sometimes one had to be creative, like a musician I know who calmly stuck pins all over his body while being interviewed by a county psychiatrist. Others quietly urinate on themselves during psychiatric evaluations. Until the '80s, you could just be your everyday freak, but now it's extremely hard: expect to be turned down on your first try, and don't try to manufacture symptoms, be they physical or mental. Nobody likes a scammer, especially the clear-eyed bullshit detectors down at the Federal Building. When I told them I was incapable of joining the work force, a panel of experts was happy to corroborate.

Medical Test Subject

Though there is a growing movement to stop medical tests involving animals, there is not such a movement to stop the lucrative use of humans in all kinds of scientific inquiry. One of my favorite bands, Daddy, has been in eight tests, stopping short of experiments on their talented brains. Pippi, a flamboyant drag queen, spent two months eating health food while her every emission was closely examined. She got a free place to stay, a much-needed vacation from her intoxicating club life, and four thousand bucks!

The director Robert Rodriguez funded his first film, *El Mariachi*, with $9,000 he got from participating in a medical test. There is one troubling experiment I wouldn't recommend — they give you as much speed as you want, but you will have nobody to talk to as you, closely observed through a one-way mirror, sink further and further into a paranoid state of dementia. A friend recently investigated the tempting back-of-the-weekly-newspaper offer to "Smoke pot, get paid!" which sounds so much more benign.

Drugs
Advice from Jennifer Blowdryer

All right. If you do not do enough drugs, you'll never understand some of the world's most important songs and stories. There is also the conversational lull that can only be filled by exchanging tales of drug experiences. Where would I be if I hadn't smoked crack? Tongue-tied and speechless, that's where. I smoked it three times and enjoyed not the drug so much as the experiences surrounding the drug; it's a great reducer of class and race division. Try it. If you get a habit though, here's how it will be on the different drugs.

Heroin You will have to be talked about a lot. "Junkie" is one of those words, like "thief," that are impossible to fully refute once you've been labeled as such. I've been stuck with both monikers at different times. "Thief! Junkie!" they will cry, before having you escorted out. This is not the real deterrent; it just hurts for a second, but provides years' worth of anecdotes. That damn methadone program is the real deterrent. Your hands'll puff up, so will you, and you'll be shaky. The government has compounded their liberal use of a toxic war drug with a punishment that is particularly hard for night people: You have to go pick up that methadone in the morning. Every morning.

Speed At first you'll be cute and chatty. You'll be confident and see connections everywhere, which passes the time on long car rides. Julie Burchill says punk rock could not have started if speed didn't make lower-class British people feel just as good... no, *better*... than the upper classes. After you get that speed habit, though, you'll resemble a reptile, I think because it is aimed at the reptilian section we retain in our brains. Our brains never really changed, just added on, and when we hit that reptile section too hard our faces become covered with diamonds of tiny wrinkles, our tongues begins to flick around, our concerns are reduced to sex and survival. One might even stomp around and break a vintage lamp, like a certain individual who will remain unnamed.

Pot Ughhh. A few days of giggling relaxation are good. By all means smoke pot, especially if you have the virus, hypertension, or some other complicated medical condition. If you are relatively healthy and smoke a lot for a long time, though, you will become the worst bore on the planet. You might even sit across from your girlfriend at breakfast just speechlessly gazing at the air — there is no worse sin.

Ecstasy It's a pretty good drug. Stop after you fall in love with a few strangers, because if you continue to do ecstasy you won't have those same good honest conversations you had at first — you'll become a smiling bore (see "Pot" above).

Acid People who have done a lot of acid tend to have the same sense of humor as me, which I like. People who did it every day for years and even shot acid might stand in the supermarket just staring at the food items for hours. This doesn't mean you need to avoid their company, just don't send them down Aisle 6 for bread. This is very complicated for them. Their brain has been exposed to too many possibilities, apparently, and can no longer function at the "Rye bread, $2.89, good price" level. Are you willing to give that up?

Prescription Drugs Prescription drugs have saved my ass, but I avoid some types. Once I found a hundred Xanax in a dead guy's apartment, but I cannot afford that kind of high. My meds are to get me up and running, not dull, flat, and lovey-dovey. I would sooner do heroin, where you start out lovey-dovey, possibly promising to send a postcard but never following through, and end up bitchy with a wobbly voice, high-pitched and melodramatic.

Drug Warning All the booze in the world will not help you write like Charles Bukowski, likewise heroin and William Burroughs or Jim Carroll. You are not as bright as them.

A Brand New You:
Tips for Surviving Rehab
Advice from Phillip R. Ford

Trendy people are known for their jaded cynicism and ironic detachment, but rehab only works if you're earnest. You might as well approach it with the right attitude, since it isn't any fun and you really don't want to do it twice. Being clean and sober is very chic right now, but even if it wasn't it would still be worth the effort — but only if you've indeed had your fill of boozing and doping. If you haven't sunk as low as you can go, there's no point in bothering with rehab. This is advice for those who are sincerely ready to join the conspicuous teetotaling ranks of virtuous celebrities like The Red Hot Chili Peppers and Janeane Garafalo.

Who am I to tell you about rehab? Well, in 1997, after eighteen years of a progressively more harrowing methamphetamine addiction, I found myself in a short bus rolling down Highway 280 with a snaggle-toothed homie named Derique on my way to my first (and so far only) term in a drug and alcohol treatment facility.

"Don't worry," he said. "It's kind of like going to camp." Derique had been there before. (I also found out later that at twenty-seven he had fathered something like ten children and had been selling crack his whole life.) Unlike a lot of people who started at the top — the Betty Ford Clinic or those television-friendly resort-like centers nestled in the foothills of the Sonoma wine country — I started at the bottom: a six-week program for indigent men in a rural/suburban setting funded by the Department of Social Services.

Turn Yourself In

Don't wait for your relatives or the law to do it for you. If you make it to the intake and are mortified and run away, you can always go back and try again. I went several times to the intake at a seedy homeless "drop-in center" before I finally submitted to treatment. A short, hairy, reformed-junkie biker-type counselor/van driver named Slick explained to me that Serenity Glen (not its real name) was a "confrontational program", and when I tried to ask questions there was a definite we're-asking-the-questions-here tone to the whole affair. I fled back to my Tenderloin hotel room, making a quick stop at my dealer's house for some yellow crank to calm me down.

Three-and-a-half years of daily meth injections, two evictions, a few weeks of homelessness, Hepatitis B, pneumonia, and the loss of all my worldly possessions and most of my friends had not been enough for me. It took six more months, an intervention, a car accident, a deforming case of chicken pox, the imminent loss of my job, and another eviction before I was ready to check in.

"Who referred you?" asked the intake counselor. They couldn't believe that I was just turning myself in. I learned later that fifty percent of Serenity Glen's clients had been remanded by drug court, and the rest had been referred directly from detox centers, hospitals and psychiatric facilities. By turning myself in, I avoided a criminal record and a tiresome association with the criminal justice system.

Don't Believe Everything People Say

I was encouraged to bond with my fellow rehabituals, but many, if not most, were career criminals and hardened liars. Every night at seven o'clock we were herded into the multi-purpose room and required to share our stories in a sad simulation of a genuine recovery meeting. The men bragged endlessly about their sordid lifetimes of unsavory misadventure: endless parades of cruelty, bad choices, sexual compulsion, brutality, double lives, violence, self-aggrandizement, granny slapping, and whore-cunt-lapping.

After a while the showing off became fascinating, if shocking. One of my favorite old guys, Bert, told the story about how in 1948 he was running though a corn field fleeing a policeman, and Bert said, "I didn't feel like going to jail that day, so I shot him." I loved that. And another guy told the story about how, as a drunken teen, he set his parents' house on fire and burned up his father. He professed it was an accident but I'm pretty sure it was on purpose. After hearing all these alarming and appalling stories, I didn't know what to believe anymore. The staff just continued urging us to trust and bond with each other. Mercy!

We all had to have a job so Mike, a fat, nerdy guy who'd spent time in the Navy, showed me the intricacies of the laundry-room routine. He told me he'd been a multi-millionaire software designer with a trophy wife but had gotten busted for smoking crack in his luxury car in Golden Gate Park. I believed him until one day he was kicked out when someone accused him of stealing five dollars, which made me wonder about his story.

Avoid Emotional Entanglements

You may be accustomed to wanton sex in the bushes or whirlwind romances, but there are rules against such things in rehab, and transgressing them can get in the way of your recovery. Temptation, though, is sure to present itself. In my case, I was pursued by an elderly African American gentleman named Monroe Wagner. He'd lost his dentures in jail, and so at mealtimes he was placed at the head of the line because it took him so long to chew his food without teeth. Monroe often would sidle up to me from behind. I thought it was kind of cute and would try to make conversation, pretending he wasn't trying to put the make on me. "What did you do before you came here?" I'd ask, cheerily.

"Shoot dope. Rob people," was the cheery reply.

My advice to you is: better to be chaste than to be chased.

Keep Your Sense of Humor

You never knew what was going to happen in Serenity Glen. At some point, a dumpy, angry Dead-heady little queen who "knew who I was" in the outside world (I had been slightly famous in an underground way for a year or two before my downfall) arrived. He called himself Yank and followed me everywhere, jabbering non-stop, quoting campy movies and such. I couldn't get rid of him.

One day my counselor called me into his office. He had another counselor on the phone and he told me that someone (some straight homophobe, I am sure) had accused me of having sex with Yank in the bushes. I just laughed and laughed.

"They both deny it," the counselor said into the phone. Apparently they believed us because the only result was that Yank and I were "put on a contract," which meant that we couldn't talk to each other, which was fine with me. Whenever Yank continued trying to babble to me about some queeny thing, I would just say, all Rhonda Penmark-ish, "You're on a contract. You're not supposed to talk to me." If I hadn't laughed it off, if I'd taken myself seriously and been a boiling pot of rage like some of the other residents, I would have gotten myself expelled and ended up back on the streets.

Bring Plenty of Money and Cigarettes

Simple pleasures mean so much when one is institutionalized, voluntarily or not. Every Saturday, a lucky few of us were selected to go into town, where we could buy whatever we wanted. That I could have all the cigarettes, cookies, and skin care products I desired was soothing to my shattered nerves. Sadly, nail polish and pornography were not allowed. Thanks to the kindness of a pair of benefactors who wanted me to succeed at recovery, I had all the petty cash I needed. The program served decaf coffee but there was a Pepsi machine; it was great to be able to buy four or five of those a day to stay awake.

The problem, though, was that I was apparently the only resident in the program with unlimited cigarettes. Every time I lit one up, and I smoked a heck of a lot back then, nineteen people asked me for a cigarette. At first I gave them out freely, but soon it became clear that I couldn't possibly give away a whole pack every time I wanted to enjoy a smoky treat, so my policy became to turn down each and every request. I would calmly explain my dilemma fifty times a day as I chain-smoked on the front steps. I felt bad, but what could I do?

Learn to Play Spades

As I said, a lot of these men had spent time behind bars, and I guess Spades is the number-one form of recreation among the incarcerated, because these fellows were quite crazy about the game. After dinner, when we were supposed to be doing the exercises in the Hazelden workbooks they gave us, the guys would break up into little groups for very intense sessions of Spades. They seemed deeply passionate about the game, and of course were hyper-competitive. I tried to get someone to teach me how to play, but forget it. If you don't know, they don't have time to teach you, that's for sure.

The people who couldn't master Spades ended up playing Uno, a game for six-year-olds that involves matching colors, shapes, and numbers. Unpleasant? I counted the days until I could get out of there, which was a mistake. I'm good with math, and so on any given day I could calculate that I was, say, X percent through my 42-day program. That made it seem even longer.

Don't Try to Go Back to Your Old Life

When re-entering trendy society, if you try to pick up where you left off, your chances of success in recovery are slim to none. Some people leave rehab and go back to their jobs as clean-and-sober bartenders, but I don't recommend it. You need to start fresh. You don't want to end up like Max Wright, the dad from *Alf*, who videotaped himself smoking crack from a beer can on his couch with two homeless dudes and had the photos show up in the *National Enquirer*. You can't just step overnight into the serene lives of recovery paragons like Margaret Cho and Elton John. I recommend a secondary program. When my 42 days were up, I thought I could go back to my old life, but then I realized I didn't have one. I moved into a Halfway House for Homosexuals (that story is another thing altogether, Mary). It worked for me.

The names and locales have been changed in order to protect the anonymity of the cases detailed above.

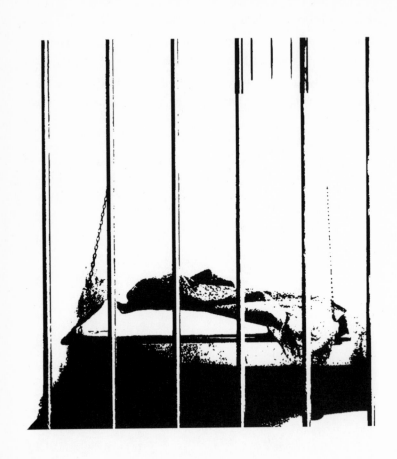

Prison Do's and Don'ts
Advice from Regi Alsin

I asked lifer Regi Mentle, a.k.a. Regi Alsin, who is at the North Kern State Men's Colony in California, for some tips on surviving in jail. This is his thoughtful reply.

Arrival

When you first come to prison you have to fill out questionnaires about your personal history. When the authorities ask if you've ever used drugs or alcohol, lie like hell cuz they'll use it against you and you'll be judged by it forever. They thrive on any idea they can think of to prove themselves better.

The next thing you need to do is leave the streets behind. Do not try to run the lives of people out there who still love you. Do not demand visits, money, or letters. Consider it a blessing that you get anything.

Visits

If someone drags their ass all the way to your prison and stands for hours to see you, it means they love you and you're blessed. Don't exploit them. This one guy had his own grandmother smuggle in drugs. She is now doing time too cuz she got caught. The worst thing about it is that he was due to get out in sixty days. Couldn't he wait?

Gossip

When someone says some guy is this or that piece of shit because of whatever, you can always respond thusly: "Okay, come say it to his/her face in front of me so we can both hear the response." If he won't, it's a good sign the gossip's not true, in which case you have to decide how close you want to be to someone who spreads falsehoods. What'll he be saying about you?

Family

Love them with every atom of your being. Get an education so they can be proud of you. Learn a trade instead of wasting your time hanging out with losers. Go to the library. Start a program of study and discovery. Use your time to become a better human being. Take up a hobby and send gifts to your relatives.

Judging

Sit back and watch. The first people who come up to you on any yard are the last people you want anything to do with. Don't put much stock in anyone who calls you "homeboy" unless you grew up with them and they're from your home area. They'll try to scam you into believing you're part of their crowd, and then they'll use you. Get wise to their games cuz they're just sizing you up as a possible victim.

Appearance

If you plan to walk the mainline, you gotta go in as hard as you can so people will know they can't just treat you any old way. On the other hand, don't be stupid and act so hard that you cause anyone to feel disrespected. Just looking "wrong" at someone with a warped ego can get you seriously hurt.

Food

Prepare to eat unhealthy garbage. If you don't have anyone on the streets who is able to send you packages or money, and you want to eat better than half-cooked beans and chicken quarters marked "not fit for human consumption", get a job.

Begging

If you're broke and nobody will send you money and you don't have a job, it's okay to bum a shot of coffee or shampoo here and there. Just don't keep hitting on the same person. Spread your hustle; come up with ways to make money like doing laundry or cleaning cells for others. You can even sew up holes in people's clothing.

War Stories

Telling detailed stories about your criminal escapades is a favorite pastime. At first these tales are pretty exciting, but after a while they weigh on your soul cuz you've heard it all a million times. Enjoy it before it becomes just another bore.

Boredom

If you've never been to prison and you complain about being bored, you need to shut the fuck up. You know nothing about boredom. Once you're here, you have to find something to do with your time and occupy your mind. I suggest something worthwhile like chess or reading every book you run across. Masturbation only lasts so long.

Tattoos

Boredom and image go hand-in-hand here. I had a cellie who tattooed a smiley face saying "Hi!" on his dick just for something to do. This one guy, "Spike", has his whole face done. He thinks it makes him hardcore. Once he started he couldn't stop. The first one, which was right in the middle of his forehead, was so bad he had to cover it up. It was a Nazi giving a salute, but it looked like a third-grade line drawing of an oil derrick with a yardarm.

If you go to a tattoo artist who thinks you're a lameass, he'll tell you one thing and do another. Some of the funniest results of this practice I know of are the guy who ended up with a giant winged penis on his back, and the little gay boy who got a unicorn whose horn was growing on the side of its head.

Drugs

Use your jail time to get off of and far away from drugs. They're dangerous out there, but even more so in here. They will kill you one way or another. Address and face the issues that caused you to turn to them in the first place.

Gambling

Some people gamble to kill time, while for others it's an addiction. I guess it can be fun but it can be dangerous, too. Some guys will spend everything they have, including money sent by someone who worked their ass off on the streets to get it for them. Some gamblers are nice; some are fucked-up bums. I've seen people call their families and manipulate money out of them with lies, telling them, "I need X amount of money to pay this debt or they'll kill me!" and then gamble the money away. Prison is a great place to learn how horribly out-of-control the human ego can get.

Respect

Not only do you need to be respectful to others, you need to think ahead about things someone might perceive as disrespect. It may be something that doesn't really matter to you, but does to someone else. Give your cellie time alone in the cell (cell time). When you brush your teeth, spit in the toilet, not the sink. And damn it, when he cums in your mouth you better swallow it!

Pride

A lot of people are proud of where they're from but put no effort into where they're going. Pride comes from accomplishment, not the color of your skin. I'm not knocking anyone who's proud of their race's accomplishments; I'm just not into politicizing it. Make your own accomplishments, too.

Whiners

Don't be a whiner. Nobody likes a whiner, not even the cops. Everyone here's going through the same shit. If you whine about everything, you're opening yourself up to abuse. Do not whine.

Sex

As in any environment without women, men eventually turn to each other in prison, but feel forced to lie about it. People stay in the closet because being a known cock-gobbler makes everyone think they have something coming, even if they are the most disgusting people you've ever met and they don't deserve anything cuz they step on you to build themselves up.

Religion

In prison, anything that makes people think they're better than everyone else ("I'm saved, you're a sinner going to Hell!") can be really dangerous. Religion can be like an alternative prison gang for punk-ass cowards.

Friends

You are gonna need friends and you're gonna have to test them to find out if they're real. Life is just a stupid game to some people, and every move they make is based on how it looks. Don't brag about what you had on the street, especially if you're lying. If you're doing a lot of time, it's extremely important to find friends. There are going to be too many people you can't even stand.

Wine

Pruno is a homemade wine that's used as an excuse to show off and get into fights. Don't be stupid and lengthen your time.

Gangs

The meanest gang is the guards, the "wall of green." Don't go up against it unless you're ready to pay the price. They can set you up and get away with anything, including killing you.

Yard Calls

Whenever someone gets into a fight or something else happens, there's a yard call where they tell all the inmates to get down. In some prisons you have to get facedown on your belly, with your face on the ground and your arms out, even in the rain and mud. If you move, the guards'll beat the shit out of you on your way to the hole.

Fights

If it comes to the point where you and another guy decide a fight is necessary, do it out of sight, like in your cell or his.

Use Your Contusions:
Mine Your Damage for Fun and Profit
Advice from Bucky Sinister

Cool kids give the impression that they were always cool. They claim to have been born with tattoos, seen The Clash when they were nine, and gotten bored with whatever you're interested in by the age of twelve. My reality was different. While my contemporaries went to all-ages shows to see the heyday of early '80s punk, I was at church camp. When they were getting drunk and listening to Black Flag, I was at an all-night prayer meeting. While they lost their virginities, wrecked cars, and were teenage miscreants, I was recruiting for my church.

My early punk scene days were rough. I was eighteen and a punk greenhorn, desperately trying to cover for myself. I knew the popular bands — Dead Kennedys, MDC, Minor Threat — but I was unaware of the smaller bands that never made it past a couple of seven-inches. I was afraid of being discovered and labeled a poseur. Soon enough, the truth came out: I was a failed fundamentalist. Instead of being ridiculed, however, just the opposite happened. I became the talk of the town. I possessed a unique and remarkable damage.

Subculture movements reward personal tragedies. Individual oppression beats demographic oppression in most circles. Most of the artists you meet will be working on group themes, rather than personal expression. While these are talented and skilled people (and I'm only slightly condescending to them now) they don't have a story to tell. They have statistics to represent, mass media news stories to reflect upon, and political trends to champion. You, as an artist of strict and authoritarian upbringing, have a story to tell, and you need to go out there and tell it. Your mission, should you choose to accept it, is to be a creator rather than a voyeur, a producer rather than a consumer.

To fully realize your artistic potential, you first need to make yourself as fascinating as possible. Here are a few tips to help you enigmatize yourself.

Watch Teensploitation Movies

Pop culture is your friend. The more pure crap you can watch, the better. Don't just watch it, study it. When your friends talk about the KISS Army, which they all claim they were in, reference the 1986 movie, *Never Too Young to Die* with Gene Simmons in drag and John Stamos, segue into the sitcom *Full House*, then mention that Bob Saget's standup act was so raunchy it made Don Rickles look like Tipper Gore. Teensploitation movies are prime ground for you. Many may watch them, but you need to declare your dedication to them loud enough for everyone in the foreign film section of the video store to hear. The late '90s era of teen trash — which delivered such gems as *10 Things I Hate*

About You, Dancer Texas, and *Jawbreaker* — is the best time for this kind of film since the mid '80s John Hughes era. While your peers bemoan the trashiness of the genre, remind them that you watch these films as if they were surreal abstractions. Three-quarters of these movies climax at the school dance. I've never seen the inside of a real school dance. I have no idea what it was like, so when I see Freddie Prinze Jr. cutting a rug to a Fatboy Slim song, it's as foreign as Fellini. The trick is reminding all your chums that while they were actually these people in high school, you were the freak who was inviting them all to Bible Study.

Fuck with Your Hair

While your friends are too jaded to get mohawks, bleach their hair, or even change the style they have, you should go no longer than six months with the same look. Inevitably, you will hear someone comment about how they had that hair in high school, which is the kind of remark I refer to as "passive condescension." Your reply should highlight the fact that your household was far too conservative for haircuts, and that your head literally would've been shaved by your Church Youth Group Leader at the church teen group's Friday night VCR double-feature of *The Computer That Wore Tennis Shoes* and *The Strongest Man in the World* (two abysmal Kurt Russell Disney movies).

Avoid Thrift Store Clothing

Thrift store clothing is the uniform of upper-class children in the Ironic Army: "Isn't this ugly?" "Yes, where DID you find it?" I didn't get any new clothes until seventh grade. That's when my dad got a raise or something, and those new clothes were from Wal-Mart. I hate wearing someone else's clothes. Proudly shop at Ross and Old Navy, and realize anyone who gives you shit probably grew up rich. Even if they didn't, your response should still be, "What?! What'd you grow up, rich or something?" The phrase will almost always shut the target down or at least put them on the defensive.

Putting It All Together

It's time to make it into a total package. At your art show, you have paintings of scenes from *The Breakfast Club* using the apostles from Da Vinci's *The Last Supper*. Bender is Judas, of course; he's the cool one. The background music is country hymns like "Walking in Sunlight" played with dulcimers and banjos, set to the lyrics of Metallica's "Unforgiven" and the *Square Pegs* theme song. You show up in a short-sleeved button-up shirt and a tie, black pants, a nametag, and your best door-knocking shoes. Pass out Mormonesque nametags to everyone. Serve tuna casserole — the staple of every fundamentalist potluck — and make sure there is something culinarily traumatic about it, like covering it with Fritos (before baking, duh) or putting raisins in it. While it's okay to make the atmosphere tacky and fun, it's most important to make your artistic statement as dark and chilling as possible. Freak 'em out a little for the ride home.

Remember to Rub It In

Guilt is the primary insecurity of the urban hipster, and thus your main tool in the fight against subcultural snobbery. Use it to your advantage. While they all rant about how much they hate organized religion, they never took part in it. Their hatred, while deserved, is largely ignorant of what you've been through. Every time a friend mentions something negative about religion, whether it's a conspiracy theory about the Vatican or an offhand poke at your neighborhood

Mormon evangelists, inform him or her that it is an insensitive comment, that it is a beliefist remark and it reminds you of something you talked about in group last week. Then go for the kill and start a declaration with, "I didn't grow up easy like you." When they insist they grew up lower-class, had hippies for parents and bought pot from their own fathers, remind them that they never dealt with corporeal punishment in grade school and were allowed to go trick-or-treating.

Picking Your Fake Name

Why fake your name? Fake names are as much a part of the trendy art world as is fake talent. If someone else is better at bad art than you are, you're going to need to one-up him or her with a better name. Local journalists for free newsweeklies — the struggling scenester's best friend — love to write about people with fake names. It makes them feel edgy, on the pulse, five minutes ahead, and all the other clichés that they swirl together in the fetid mixing bowl they call journalism.

But how to get a name? You can't just decide to switch from "Larry" to "Gravedigger". It'll never work. You'll be the joke of the town. It's scenicide. Following are two good ways to get that perfect fake name.

Band Name/Last Name

Many people with fake names were in a band, and the name of the band became their last name. This is most common with Johns, Joes, Daves, and Mikes. When someone asks, "Do you know Dave?" the other person can respond with, "Which Dave? Dave Bloodsucker or Dave Criminal?" See? Pretty cool, huh? Until your new name sticks, make sure that you do not name your band something you can't live with, such as Tinydicks, Smellycunts, Penisfarts, or Gonorrhea, all of which are great band names, but would suck as last names.

Leave Town

This is the easy way to launch a brand new name. Move to Austin, Seattle, Portland, or some such town, and just start calling yourself something. Everyone will believe you. It's easy. Pretty soon, everyone will be talking about Igby Destruction, the radical artist who just moved in off the East Coast. Trust me; it's a lot easier and faster than getting a seminal band together.

More Tips

Be sure to avoid names that are overdone. Spike, Spider, and Raven are taken. There's already someone in town by that name. If not, they've left behind a bad reputation with their overdone name. You don't need to bear the sins of a previous name-owner.

British names are easy to get away with. Ian, Angus, and Anton are commonly pulled off. Even if you're obviously not British, you can claim grandparenthood.

Classic literature, like Edgar Allan Poe's work, is ripe for name-mining. While "The Raven" should be avoided and "Lenore" has newfound popularity due to the hit comic, "Annabel Lee" is always good.

Oh, and don't forget about creative spelling — Michael becomes Mykel, Murray can take on a French symbol and become *Murree,* and, of course, the dated capitalization of proper names can be dropped – start insisting on this to add to the annoyance factor.

Employment

Unless you are lucky enough to be born a trustifarian, you will have to get a job. Don't even think of turning to drug dealing or crime. It won't work. You'll make more money minimum-waging it, and the

112

inevitable prison stint will literally destroy your life. Take as many jobs as you can get. Work the minimum amount of hours per week. You should have at least two jobs, but try to work your way up to three. You're not going to make good money anywhere, so go where the getting is good. Now, how to use crappy jobs to your advantage:

Clubs, Bars, and Concerts Working in clubs or bars is the best way to get to know the largest amount of people in the smallest amount of time. *Pros*: High visibility, free admission to shows, after-hours drinking, free/cheap drinks, easy access to drugs, and blackout romances. *Cons*: Nocturnal hours mean you will never date someone from the Daytime World, deafness, drug and alcohol addiction, and blackout romances.

Retail The employee discount, as well as the five-finger discount, makes this worthwhile. Often you will get discounts at other retail outlets. You should try to get access to cheap clothing, shoes, books, DVDs, and music. This is recommended for people who are good at looking great every waking hour. *Pros*: High visibility, discounts, occasional swag, overt rudeness. *Cons*: The worst-paying jobs available, idiot tourists and poseurs, robbery.

Behind the Scenes The discounts here are so good you don't need to steal from work but your coworkers will steal entire cases of books, records, clothes, whatever it is you're dealing in. There's always one schmuck who robs the place blind so that the boss will never relax. On this level of business, you can actually become a "player": someone who can get a band signed to a label, an author published, a DVD produced. *Pros*: Lots of swag, player status, dressing like a slob everyday, better pay than the other two categories. *Cons*: You have earned skills of the outside world, and must constantly balance your inner desires of working somewhere you love versus working somewhere you could actually make some money. Low visibility. Working in the Daytime.

Lynnee's Skool for Boyz
Advice from Lynn Breedlove

Unka Lynnee's Skool for Boyz was created for butches and transguys cuz the femmes of SF complained to Unka Lynnee, "There are no good butches in this town!" That statement is not true. There are now five, all graduates of ULSFB. This is their curriculum.

What the men don't get is: you are part girl. Oh no! Oh yeah. No shame in girliness. Deep down under all that tuff guy business, you got a squishy, emotional, compassionate heart. That's what she likes about you. She's a dyke, remember? She wants a tang-ownin' mofo who's masculine — that's her FIRST choice. She only resorts to bio men when dykes and trannies can't cut it.

Get Some Boy Pals

You're gonna need a network of support, pals who are on some kind of path themselves, and aren't just beer buddies. Femmes make great pals. Ninety percent of my closest pals are chickeebabes. You can talk to 'em about anything, and they will never shame you. Also, they'll tell you "what women really want."

Still, you gotta have some homies that you can talk about shit with, too. How you felt funny cuz you didn't know what size dick to use on the first date. Is that girl you're hot for totally sweet, or has she been known to be ridiculously jealous and unreasonable? You also need homeboiz to find out what kind of products to use, which gym has the biggest queer clientele, how to grow or remove hair, or just to check in with when you feel like a total freak.

Butch pals can share trade secrets such as packing, strapping 'em down, and favorite lubes and toyz.

Lemme Hear Your Body Talk

Be strong physically to match the mental and spiritual giant you are. The new you needs a workout, whether you're on testosterone or not. If you're not banging T, you need the gym to get muscles and not be depressed. If you are on T, you need to work out for relaxation, cuz it's bouncing you around like a ping pong ball in a Lotto air tank.

Workin' out gives you the confidence that comes from being able to kick serious ass in an emergency. It's a good feeling to know you can protect yourself and your babe. It's also nice to be able to lift up babes and pork 'em against the wall. They love that.

Self-defense for the lazy: Always keep a roll of pennies in your pocket, so if you do have to clock someone, you'll be able to do it in one punch. When an asshole gives you trouble:

1. Say "Whoa, look at that babe..."
2. Pull his head down and your knee up to smash his nose.
3. While he's grabbing his face, kick him in the balls.
4. When he goes down, kick him in the head and ribs.
5. Take off running.

Fuck fair fights. There are no fair fights between the tang-owning people and bio guys. If you fight fair, you will lose. Always be aware of your surroundings and potential threats. Be going over your five-item punch-out plan. Smile right up until the point when you clock the motherfucker. You're smaller, and you need the element of surprise. I know you're smaller, cuz most guys that attack chix, trannies, or queers are scared to pick on someone their own size.

Pronouns

"Them" is a good pronoun when you're not sure about a person's gender, as in, "Is your *partner* comin' to the party? They said they might." I also made up the pronouns "shim", a combination of she and him, and "sherm" (she, hers and him). It's not too scientific, it's more poetic and subjective, and it's a political refusal to accept the binary gender system. Shim and herm are for people who don't relate to "he" cuz they're a man-hatin' man, and don't relate to "she" cuz they're feminists but not really chicks; shim and herm are for genderqueers, and herm is also now used by intersex folks to describe themselves. A bio boy is a genetic male

She's a Sick Fuck

Find out what her fantasies are. Maybe she wants a teenage boy, or she might be into truckdrivers with topiaries creeping out from under their wife pleezers and wanna crawl thru to underbrush to give you a bj. You can always ask, or you can just look for the girl who likes the kinda guy you are.

Packing

You got two dicks, one for squishy realism in case she grabs ya, and one for boinking. The soft one's called a packie, which made of Cyberskin. You're supposed to drop 'em in your tighty-whities though, which is a problem, cuz they can fall out and, whoa — embarrassing. You just gotta keep walkin' and go buy another one. Don't even bend down and claim that shit.

My pal Sid made a soft leather harness that's just a three-inch piece of leather that snaps on the front-inside of your boxer waistband. You can sew the snaps on yourself. The piece of leather measures 3" wide at the top where it snaps and then hangs free 3" long by 2" wide down to where your dick would come out of your body. Sid cuts a hole a little smaller than the packie, then slips the packie through so it hangs there inside your boxers. Security in your pants makes for a confident guy.

For boinking, I like to get custom-made harnesses from my pal Skeeter who works at Mr. S Leather. You can go for fittings at your local leather-tooler pal's shop. They're all one piece: no bulky buckles or rings that pinch and poke to adjust. There's a big stiff triangular piece of leather in front with a hole the size of your fave dick (bring your cock to the fitting) cut in it. Three snaps around the outside of the hole can hold smaller rings, should you wanna switch out your usual schlong for a smaller tool. Sewn to the triangle are two wide elastic sections that go around your hips like a belt on the sides, attached to a T-shape of really soft garment leather that goes down your butt crack. It fits snug, like your dick is attached to your body, for maximum control.

Now you don't wanna walk around with a stiffie for the whole date cuz that looks stupid and is not comfy. You can wear the harness dickless, plus the packie if you want, and at the crucial moment, go to the can and slip your rock-hard manhood into the harness. *Et voila...* Action Jackson! Hint: you might wanna wear baggy clothes if you need to be discreet, like at a fancy restaurant.

Words of Encouragement

OK, ladeez and herms. Go forth and get some! They're lined up around the block to hump your leg.

Sherilyn's Skool for Girlz
Advice from Sherilyn Connelly

So you want to be a girl. Congratulations. Oh, you've actually always been a girl, in spite of what your body looks like? I know the feeling. Either way, you've got a long road ahead before the rest of the world figures it out. It's twisty and scary and not without its share of pitfalls, but it's not impossible either. What I do know is this: If I can use the women's restroom at the Wal-Mart in rural Nebraska and not get a second look, then so can you.

Surgery is not necessary. Being born with a penis does not mean you aren't a girl — you just can't become pregnant. Gender identity is in your mind. That said, I'm all for altering one's body to match one's mind, and have done so myself through hormones and electrolysis.

If you need a surgically-constructed vagina to make life worth living, go for it. Just remember: if your goal is to be accepted as female by the world at large, it isn't enough. The waiter who called you "Sir" yesterday will not call you "Ma'am" tomorrow just because of your neo-coochie.

Go by the book, if you can afford it. The book, such as it is, requires twelve weeks of therapy with a licensed psychologist (*mit* Ph.D.), who then writes you a letter of recommendation for the endocrinologist, who in turn writes you the actual prescription for hormones and monitors you during the process. If you're for real, it's a breeze — an irritating breeze, but a breeze nonetheless. None of this is cheap, of course, and it's not always covered by medical insurance, assuming you even have such a thing. Be prepared to hear the question, "Have you thought this through?" more than once. Answering without gritting your teeth takes a bit of practice.

Research. Read as much as you possibly can on the subject. People are going to ask you a lot of questions, so the more you know, the better prepared you'll be to answer. Be mindful of when the material was written. Many universities and major metropolitan libraries still have sexuality books from the mid-to-late twentieth century.

It's okay to feel a little - you know - down there. There's a hell of a lot of debate in the tranny community about the concept of "autogynephilia," being aroused by the thought of changing one's gender. Many deny that such a thing even exists, claiming it reduces gender dysphoria to a sexual fetish. This is a valid concern since sexuality is very much a separate issue from gender. For example, I've changed my outward gender to match my mind, but my sexuality hasn't changed; I remain as attracted to girls as ever.

Get in shape. You're going to be putting a lot of stress on your body, both physically and emotionally. Eat healthy and get plenty of exercise. If you've already been tossing around the idea of detoxing, now is the perfect time to start. The competing hormones will be overworking your liver as it is, and that poor embattled internal organ shouldn't have to contend with alcohol. Smoking does your skin no favors, and it doesn't help your voice, either.

Give people time to adjust. Allow a grace period of six months for people to start using your new name. After that, correct them as strongly as necessary without being rude. If you're rude it WILL be held against you. Never mind the utter rudeness of someone who knows better using your boy name, whether intentionally or out of carelessness. *You* are the one on trial.

Although you'll have made it clear to people that both your name and your gender have changed, and that should be glaringly obvious to anyone who looks at you, allow another six months or so for the pronouns. Get used to pronoun mistakes. Some may never quite get it.

Most women do not have high voices. So neither should you. If necessary, see a speech therapist.

Go light on the plastic surgery. Really, really light. If hormones and electrolysis have done their job, facial feminization surgery shouldn't be necessary, although this can vary dependent on genetic background.

If you feel you need to, *get only as much done as is absolutely necessary.* A reconstructed face looks like what it is. Even more so than with genetic girls, facial feminization surgery can result in a generic, Kewpie doll-ish countenance, an unnerving sameness. Put a few trannies who've had the surgery next to one another, and you'd swear you're looking at identical siblings from a family descended from European royalty. Individuality and personality is lost under unnaturally high cheekbones and big scary lips.

Unless you lost the majority of your lip tissue in a buzz saw accident, there's no need for collagen. Above all else, though, in the name of all that is good and right: NO BOTOX. Please, I'm begging you.

Electrolysis. Quite possibly the key to passing. If you have to choose between surgery and electrolysis, I suggest electrolysis. Out in the world, facial hair is a much bigger giveaway than your groin. No matter how close you shave your face, there's always that hint, that shadow. Wearing enough makeup to cover the shadow can result in unwanted attention and only works for a few hours at best.

Ideally, you'd begin electro before coming out, and certainly before going full-time. For efficiency's sake, electro requires a few days worth of beard growth, and that's a lot easier to get away with if everyone still thinks you're a boy.

Traditional electrolysis hurts a lot. After all, an electrified needle is being stuck into your skin. The pain only occurs during the session, though, and is manageable. Bring your own music along, something comforting (much as I love it, *Further Down the Spiral* by Nine Inch Nails was a really bad idea).

Avoid laser electrolysis. It simply isn't reliable enough.

Hormones. The most commonly prescribed estrogen pill for both trannies and genetic girls is Premarin. Usually it's taken in conjunction with an androgen blocker such as Spironactalone. Premarin's name is uncomfortably descriptive of its source, the urine of pregnant mares. All together now: ewwww. However, I've ingested it daily, and willingly, since 1998.

Friends. You will probably lose at least one friend, someone dear to you who decides they just can't handle it — their loss. When the dust finally settles, you'll have a much better sense of who your friends really are. You may be surprised.

Stealth. It is simply not possible to go into complete stealth. Period. Unless you go on a killing spree, somebody always knows your secret. That gives them power over you, and the potential for blackmail. Of course, blackmail only works if you consider what you're doing shameful or embarrassing. Nobody passes completely. *You will get clocked now and again.* The ability to say "Yeah, I was born a boy, so the hell what?" is your best defense.

Your name. Even if you haven't come out to anyone, you probably already know your name. It's one of the most satisfying aspects of transitioning, and one of the most personal. It's also one of the only things you can really control; when I started out, all I knew was that whatever else happened, my name would be Sherilyn Connelly.

The Joy of Debt
Advice from Mykel Board

The Right Mindset

If you die in debt, you win. You've spent money you didn't have, bought things you couldn't afford, gone places you couldn't get to and done things you couldn't do. If you die rich, you lose. You leave all that wasted potential. Where did it get you? Are you any less dead than a poor man? You missed everything you could have done with that money. Understanding this basic principle moves us to the logical question: *How can I get myself in maximum debt and live like a celebrity while doing it?*

Credit cards are the banks' way of saying WE WANT TO GIVE YOU MONEY. Banks compete, falling over themselves to serve you. They beg you to take their money, giving you presents, discounts, and special offers, if only you'll take their money. It would be rude to disappoint them.

Don't let talk about *fees* and *interest* and *penalties* put you off debt. You've got to change your way of thinking. You are NOT paying interest. You are NOT paying back a loan. You are paying $50 a month so EVERYTHING IS FREE. The only reason to care about interest rates is that they bring you closer to the villain of our story, your credit limit. There is no debtor's prison in the U.S., so even if things go massively wrong, they can't lock you up.

Starting on the Great Path to Indebtedness

If you're just starting out, you have NO CREDIT HISTORY. This is the number one reason for being rejected for a credit card.

But *you* won't have that problem if you get a credit card while you're in college. Banks like to throw money at college students. They have the best collateral: PARENTS. If you have a college credit card, make sure you pay it back slowly, about ten percent a month, until it reaches zero. Now you're ready for your other cards.

Not in college? Easy, just come up with $500. If you have drug connections, are excessively attractive, or have parents who REALLY love you, getting that $500 without resorting to work should be easy.

You'll never spend this money. It's an investment you make to get a SECURED credit card. Secured cards look like Visas or MasterCards, but there's a catch. You need enough money in the bank to cover your credit limit; a $500 deposit will get you a $500 limit on your card. Once you get the card, go out and spend. Don't charge up the whole kit and caboodle the first day. It doesn't look good. Spend about $100 a month to start the cash rolling. Don't charge groceries, booze, or other necessities; it makes the banks think you don't have an income. Only use the card to buy what is absolutely useless.

Remember: use a high-interest card with perks like frequent flyer miles to buy things, then transfer the balance to a low interest card to pay it back. You should be all right for a year with your first two credit cards. When you're comfortable, tell the bank to cancel the secured card. You won't need it anymore. Keep that $500 in the bank, though. You'll need it later.

How to Use Your Credit Cards to Pay the Rent and Buy Stuff

You can use credit cards to pay for ANYTHING: rent, drugs, whores, bail, the damages to your downstairs neighbor's stereo when you nodded out while the bathtub was filling. Using credit cards for these things takes some ingenuity, but you can do it. If you weren't creative, you'd have a job. Right?

DON'T turn your credit cards into cash through "cash advances". Why? First, you don't get airline miles or "bonus points" for cash advances. Second, the interest rate on those advances is more than twenty percent. Third, cash advances bring you closer to your credit limit with no frivolous luxuries to show for it.

So why not get the cash from what SOMEONE ELSE buys? That way, you get the lower purchase interest *and* the frequent flyer miles. The easiest way to do this is at a bar or restaurant. Bring your friends. Eat, drink and be merry. At the end of the night, pay the entire bill with your credit card. Your friends pay you cash. Bingo! Instant dollars and frequent flyer miles, just for having a good time.

When It All Collapses

If you're lucky (and most are), you'll die before there is any trouble. The joke will be on the banks. Let 'em try to get $120,000 out of a few pickled pounds of rotting meat.

If you're unlucky, ALL your cards will be in the NO CHARGE ZONE (somewhere way past their credit limits). And those pre-approved offers won't be pre-approved anymore. If you keep track, keep up your minimum payments, and keep getting more cards, you'll have ten to fifteen years of riding high before this happens. If you're unlucky and live some extra years, it's NO BIG DEAL. Remember, THERE IS NO DEBTOR'S PRISON IN AMERICA.

One solution is to go directly into bankruptcy. That's quick, but you still have to go through paying a lawyer and getting counseling, and you end up with seven years of bad credit rating. The $500 you saved from your first card will pay the lawyer. But can you go seven years without a credit card? Think about that before you jump on the bankruptcy bandwagon.

Another option is *credit counseling*. I have no idea why they call it that. There is no counseling and you LOSE your credit. Still, it can help. You've seen the ads on the TV you bought with your Delta Skymiles card. These companies consolidate your debts, lower your monthly interest payments, stop over-the-limit and late fees, and combine everything into one lump monthly payment.

Before they start on your case, they'll ask you for the outstanding charges on ALL your credit cards. LIE! While you're under their plan you cannot use your cards. That would destroy your life, or at least your lifestyle. By now, you should have at least eight credit cards. Keep the one with the MOST SPACE between the current charges and the credit limit. If they're *all* maxed out, keep the one with the lowest interest rate. You'll have to pay that one separately from the credit counseling deal, but at least you'll have a credit card.

Under the counseling plan, you'll pay your other cards off in five years. It'll cost around $500 a month. After that, you start with a fresh set of credit cards. Then you go another ten to fifteen years, living the high life, and, if you're lucky, dying before you have to start again.

The Black Friend
Advice from Brother Man X

Brother Man X is the pseudonym chosen by one of my favorite New York comedians. He has generously offered up this tongue-in-cheek advice on the topic of the Black Friend.

Having a Black Friend: Why It's Important

It's real simple. There're only so many times you can go to Zanzabar or Spa Bar, before that shit becomes the WASPiest hangout in America. You wanna at least hang with the Negroes. Black America knows what's going on in New York for everybody with at least some singe of suntan around their face. At least get some culture. That's what New York's about. I mean, come on, shit.

It's like that moment in class on Martin Luther King Day and everybody's wondering what Martin Luther King would say on a day like this. *Well since he's dead, how about Rae Kwan over here*, and so you gotta be the spokesman for Black America. It's odd as fuck. Everybody needs some kinda color.

White Friends

I've got white friends cuz there's only so much forty-ounce drinking you wanna do. White friends keep good weed. Seriously. I have not met a good white friend who smokes seeds and stems. I can always get a bag of shake, but the white people be keeping all the KB (Kind Bud) and shit for themselves. It's amazing. I don't know where y'all get it from.

I can't catch no cab without the white man throwing his hand out, or the chick acting like she's gonna run out in Fourteenth Street. That's why I employ my white friends and associates.

Choosing Your Black Friend

The Negro comes in many shapes, forms and sizes. You'll find us at the library, and you'll find us at the liquor store. We're everywhere. It all depends on the kind of Negro you're comfortable with. The first thing you need to do is decide what type of Black friend you're looking to hang out with. There are four types:

Type A This is the kind you're gonna meet at school. For the most part, America is about opportunity. So once you get yourself to the university of your choice, you're gonna meet the "I bust my ass to get up in here, there's no financial aid" type of Negro. That's the first kind of Black person that most people meet outside of Brandon in your sixth grade class.

The college Negro is gonna be OK. There's gonna be a lot of hating of the beer, because Black folks do not drink much beer. Some of us do, but that's, like, at cookouts. Other than that, the benefits of having the college Negro as a friend are solid.

It's not that the brother has more personality, it's just different. I mean, shit, you been hanging out watching *Party of Five* all day, wouldn't you like to hang out with somebody who been watching *The Jeffersons* the whole goddamn day?

Type B This is the type that didn't go to school at all. Round-the-way mothafuckas. If you hang around that kind of crowd, chances are all the shit you see and hear on the news will happen to you. Some people still do seek this out but, hey, you get what you pay for. I keep in close contact with folks like this, but outside of my weed, and what the fuck is going on in the block, that's all I need to know. I keep moving. I don't wanna be your alibi.

Type C He didn't go to school, but he had enough sense to get his plumber's license. He smokes a little, drinks a little, got a little rap sheet, but it's nothing serious, maybe a DUI, it didn't hurt nobody. It is what it is. That's the easiest Black person to meet, because that motherfucker is in your building. His washer and dryer is coming through your fucking roof. You'll see him everyday. In fact, he'll feel reassured since you're around, like, "I can see that niggers haven't infiltrated this spot." You see, white people are like policemen on horseback. You know that you're gonna be all right because if something goes down, somebody's gonna be calling the cops, and it ain't gonna be us. It's a good thing sometimes.

The advantage of Type C is that he'll allow you to see the kind of Negroes that he works out with. There are Blacks that he hangs out with, there are Blacks he doesn't hang out with, and then there's his family. Shit, he can't pick 'em. There might be a pedophile in there, there might be a professor in there. It's an educational thing. Look at how they live.

135

Type D These are the knuckleheads. There's nothing you can do for these cats. You definitely don't need to go making friends with the crackhead on the corner. Not even in passing. No. Wrong. All they can do is basically serve as the mirror that you don't wanna be looking at. You don't want that type of friend. I'm not saying you shouldn't throw a couple quarters here and there, you know, "there but for the grace of God go I." If he just wants to shoot that shit up, there's nothing I can do. That relationship ain't going nowhere unless he's selling the ILLEST weed, and most of the time he ain't cuz he's moved up to the fifth floor of drugs so he's like, "Fuck weed!"

Fuck that, you'll get tuberculosis, listen to what your parents say. I'm from a sensible line of thinking. I ain't gonna chill on the block when I got an apartment with cable in it. This is your worst type of Negro friend.

Forging the Friendship

You gotta let it come. We're just not that outgoing. You gotta be comfortable, like, "He's all right. He's seen me drunk and shit,Ó or, "She's OK, she was holding my weed while the cops was out here and shit." Hey, you know, boom, you pay us a favor or some shit like that, we can associate with you, you know what I mean? You're not a cornball, you know what's going on. You gotta show some street smarts.

Any Black friend who allows a white friend to see his house, that's a good sign there. Any Black friend who hasn't let you see his house, he's probably asking himself every day, "How cool is this muthafucka?" It takes some time. We're coming from a society where we just don't trust y'all. It's not that I don't care, it's just, you know, exactly *how* close is this mothafucka to the police. I know *you're* not. I'm not talking about you.

Some of the Mistakes that White People Make in Trying to Befriend Black People

Turning on the music and start dancing on the spot. That's wrong, you all need to stop that shit. It's archaic. You need to calm down.

Another faux pas is to straight-up just start rhyming and everything like that, or asking Black people's opinions on rap music. Like hey, hey, hey, hey, calm the fuck on down, you know what I'm saying. Maybe I've got a *Maroon 5* CD up in my shit, maybe not. You gotta scout out people. I scout out all my white friends. I gotta see if you got Negro tendencies. You know? Or likable Negro tendencies. Got his own house. Graduated. Knows what the fucking deal is. It is what it is.

Another thing to stay away from is saying shit like, "My homeboy, my nigga." It takes a while. There are some white folks out there who can kind of use the term "nigga." But the thing is, they've been jumped in by their group. Then some white cat's just high and says "Let this nigga handle it." Then the mothafucka's like "Did I just say that?" Shit, you been around enough, now come on, you need to get the fuck on out.

Fabulous Hints
Advice from the Know-It-All, Jane King

Jane King started out in Santa Cruz, and has since lived in several cities. Once people in a certain place get too dependent on her advice, she must move on — from Austin, to Madrid, to Chicago, to New York, London, then New York again. She is flawlessly beautiful and travels quite light. "Just throw that thing away," she has often advised me, "because you can always get another one if you need it."

Smoking It's true that smoking cigarettes does make you slightly thinner. They set up an internal vibration that causes you to burn calories. You can feel the internal vibration go away between two and eight months after you quit. They are also fun to put in your mouth. There are times when you feel like that specific kind of mouth event, rather than the chewing kind.

BUT THEY ARE TERRIBLE FOR YOUR SKIN. My friend Sharon gave up cigarettes when she was thirty, mainly because she noticed they had turned the skin around her mouth yellow. Then she took them back up again when she was forty-four for a couple of years, during which time the pores on her face, particularly right around her mouth, went from flawless to rather coarse. Now, she has to have her skin laser-resurfaced. If you smoke long enough, you will get small lines everywhere and deep lines above your upper lip (which is from drawing in — smoking is a sign of not being fulfilled and means "I need. I need."), but you can also get giant pores all over your face, as if you have had bad acne.

Also, if you smoke, you can't get much plastic surgery, because you won't heal very well. Many of the ultra-luxe recovery hotels won't even let someone in if they smoke. I mean, how serious is that? They refuse to take your money.

Plastic Surgery Plastic surgery is a really good idea. The main thing to do is figure out exactly what you need. Everyone ages differently. Some people have absolutely no wrinkles at ninety. That doesn't mean they look like they're thirty, it just means that wrinkles are not the problem. You could be dealing with jowls, dewlaps, and puffiness around the eyes instead. These are all things that can be fixed. Take a very close look at your face. Do you have lines coming from the corners of your mouth down toward your chin? (Disapproval lines, I call them. I have them.) These can be fixed with collagen injections. It's also a good idea to have Botox injected to keep you from continuing to pull your mouth down.

When I first started getting collagen injections, I became aware of the facial expressions I was using and tried to stop making them. For example, I'd been holding my mouth tense when I was around other people. When I became aware of this, I consciously relaxed my mouth and unsurprisingly discovered a great side benefit, in that I was much more comfortable socially. Later I got Botox between my brows and experienced a similar phenomenon. A slight tenderness alerted me whenever I was *frowning in consternation* and when I stopped making the expression, the emotion also disappeared.

Tipping Tipping is very important and reveals who you are. You must tip very well all the time unless the service is purposefully bad. I know almost all the money-savers out there like to leave skimpy little tips, simply because it is not a mandatory expense. This is a terrible mistake. Here are the reasons why:

1) People who receive tips for their work often connect their self-esteem to the amount you tip them. In a situation where you have spent, oh, say, five dollars and the appropriate tip would be one dollar, if you leave fifty cents, you have saved yourself a little money but have also made another human feel like shit. If, on the other hand, you give two dollars instead, the spirits of the other human will soar. Isn't a dollar worth it? What else can you possibly spend that money on that will get you so much for so little?

2) Waiters and waitresses grow up to be other things like the head of multinational corporations where you want jobs, or beautiful models and actors who you want to date. They remember. They might not remember exactly how you tipped (although some can), but they always carry a FEELING about you around. You're going to feel like an idiot when you don't get to be senior vice president of the Whatsis Corporation because you insisted on saving fifty cents. Which reminds me - never tip less than a dollar, you just look like a boob.

About the Authors

Alvin Orloff is the author of two novels: *I Married an Earthling* and *Gutter Boys*, both published by Manic D Press. He lives in San Francisco and is currently working on his third, fourth, and fifth novels. He is also available for weddings and bar mitzvahs.

Pamela Holm's essays have been published in *The San Francisco Chronicle*, *The Denver Post*, *San Francisco Magazine*, FreshYarn.com, and various other publications. Her memoir *The Toaster Broke, So We're Getting Married*, originally published in hardcover with MacAdam/Cage, has recently been released in paperback by Villard Books. Pamela's first novel, *The Night Garden*, is forthcoming from MacAdam/Cage.

Ariel Gore's books include the vagabond memoir *Atlas of the Human Heart* and the parenting classics *The Hip Mama Survival Guide*, *The Mother Trip & Whatever*, and *Mom: Hip Mama's Guide to Raising a Teenager*. Her website is www.arielgore.com.

Sherilyn Connelly (sherilynconnelly.org) is a San Francisco-based writer. She has read her work at many California events including K'vetch, The Unhappy Hour, Siren, Poetry Mission, and Ladyfest Bay Area. More of her sentences can be found in *Holy Titclamps*, as well as *I Do/I Don't: Queers on Marriage* (Suspect Thoughts). Her theatrical forays include acting in stage productions of *Night of the Living Dead*, *The Hitchhiker's Guide to the Galaxy* and "Zippy the Pinhead" (as Karen Carpenter), in addition to adapting and directing a live-action *Twilight Zone* episode.

Clint Catalyst is the author of the speed-addled memoir *Cottonmouth Kisses* (Manic D Press) and co-editor of the anthology *Pills, Thrills, Chills and Heartache: Adventures in the First Person* (Alyson Books). His writing has appeared in the *LA Weekly*, *SF Bay Guardian*, *Instinct*, *Surface*, *Hustler*, and *Swindle*, among other publications. He lives in Los Angeles, where he pens a column for the *LA Alternative Press* entitled "Antics & Semantics."

Jane King: When my brothers and I were young, we were very interested in catching bees. Our idea was that when bees would land on our hands, we would run so fast to the house, where my mother was waiting with a glass jar, that the bee would not have time to sting us. Unfortunately, no matter how quickly we worked, we always got stung. One day, while we were°engaged in this game, the doorbell rang and my mother answered to find a Welcome Wagon woman. She offered the woman cake and they started chatting. After a while though, my mother noticed that the woman looked uncomfortable and she asked if something was wrong. "Well, I was just wondering about your children. Aren't you worried about them?" Only then did my mother tune in to the chorus of small, "Ouch, ouch" pause "ouch, ouch," that was coming from outside. "Oh don't worry," my mother quickly said. "They're just out there catching bees."

Mykel Board believes: if you're going to do something right, why bother doing it at all? An exception to this is getting into both debt and trouble. These are two things he's been doing for longer than most of this book's readers have been alive. Mykel has published seventeen novels, including *Hot Firemen in Drag, Switch Hitting Teens* and *Slit Slappers*. Two other books are in the works. One is a collection of his twenty+ years of columns in *Maximum Rock'n'Roll*, to be called *I, A Me-ist* and published by Hope and Nothings Press in Chicago, before the next millennium. The other is a memoir of his time in Mongolia, *Even A Daughter Is Better Than Nothing*. It is also scheduled for second millennium publication.

Bucky Sinister is the author of *Whiskey and Robots* (Gorsky) and *King of the Roadkills (Manic D)*. He failed at various social scenarios before arriving in San Francisco, where social failure is a trend in and of itself.

Jim Flynn interviewed Brother Man X, Moonshine, and Nate from Frisco Tattoo. He is a relocated suburban kid who prides himself on his complete ignorance of trendiness and all of its accoutrements. For the past three years he walked around downtown with a pack of cigarettes and a microphone recording *Stranger to the System: Life Portraits of a New York City Homeless Community*, a collection of the life stories of twenty people living on the streets of the Lower East Side. Check out this and other New York tales at curbsidepress.com.

Regi Mentle grew up in San Bruno, California as Dennis Alsin, bastard son of Robert Wayne Dolph (who doesn't even know about Dennis) and Patricia Clark-Alsin. Dennis was a fat, poor, ugly welfare brat and was already that way when punk rock happened, so it was perfect for him. He actually believed it was the thing that would take over. Now he says it is a failure because it didn't change a thing.

It sure was fun, though. After four years of mad drug abuse to the beat, going back and forth between the San Francisco and Los Angeles punk scenes making a living selling MDA, he ended up going too far. When a guy tried to kill him on Broadway in SF with a Swiss Army knife, Dennis took the knife from him and stabbed him to death.

He has presently served twenty-four years on a sentence of fifteen, and should have been released in 1990. Write to Regi at this address: Regi Alsin C-38627, Box 8103-5146, SLO, CA 93409-8103.

Reverend Jen is an elf-eared author, performance artist, visual artist, upcoming celebrity/personality, underground movie star, Troll Museum founder and curator, Voice of the Downtrodden and Tired, and Patron Saint of the Uncool. She is the author of many fine books including *Sex Symbol for the Insane* and *Reverend Jen's Really Cool Neighborhood*. She writes for her own magazine, *Art Star Scene* (ASS) and www.nerve.com. Currently she lives in her Troll Museum on the Lower East Side with Saint Reverend Jen Junior, a chihuahua.

James St. James, who was once dubbed a "celebutante" by *Newsweek* magazine, now leads a quiet, sedate existence in Los Angeles, far from the madness he writes about. He has kindly allowed use of an excerpt from his book *Party Monster*, which has been made into a major motion picture you really should see.

Phillip R. Ford is a once-noted entertainer and stage and film director whose projects include the classic cult film *Vegas in Space*. He now works as a middle-manager for one of the world's largest financial services corporations.

Editor **Jennifer Blowdryer**, a.k.a. Jennifer Waters, got her dumb name from The Blowdryers, a punk band she was in as a teen. She is a former columnist for *Maximum Rock'n'Roll*, and currently writes for *New York Press*. She is the author of *Modern English: A Photo-Illustrated Trendy Slang Dictionary*, *The Laziest Secretary in the World*, and *White Trash Debutante*, and co-founded the new literary movement Spectacularist International and its house organ, *Persiflage*. She currently lives in Manhattan, and dreams of visiting your town with a small panel of experts.

Acknowledgements

Thanks to Alvin Orloff who helped a great deal with editing certain chapters, Michael Louie for editorial assistance, my hairdresser Princess Kennedy, Kevin Killian and Dodie Bellamy, my mother Lenore who always has something good for me to read, the Bowery Poetry Club for being my hangout spot, my NYC assistant Brooke Lockyer, the Department of Agriculture, Ann Davies for listening, and all my contributors.

Photo Credits: Rev Jen, Moonshine, Mykel Board: Amy Chace; Bucky Sinister, Lynn Breedlove, Nate, Erno, Zeon: Uncle Tim; Jennifer Blowdryer: Randal Alan Smith; Brother Man X: Jim Flynn; Alvin Orloff: Brook Dillon; Clint Catalyst: Andrea Ferrante.